CAMBRIDGE MUSIC HANDBOOKS
Bach: The Goldberg Variations

Many listeners and players are fascinated by Bach's *Goldberg Variations*. In this wide-ranging and searching study, Professor Williams, one of the leading Bach scholars of our time, helps them probe its depths and understand its uniqueness. He considers the work's historical origins, especially in relation to all Bach's *Clavierübung* volumes and late keyboard works, its musical agenda and its formal shape, and discusses significant performance issues.

In the course of the book he poses a number of key questions. Why should such a work be written? Does the work have both a conceptual and a perceptual shape? What other music is likely to have influenced the *Goldberg*? and to what extent is it trying to be encyclopedic? What is the canonic vocabulary? How have contemporaries or musicians from Beethoven to the present day seen this work and, above all, how has its mysterious beauty been created?

PETER WILLIAMS is John Bird Professor at Cardiff University and Arts and Sciences Distinguished Chair Emeritus at Duke University. His publications include *The Organ Music of J. S. Bach* volumes I, II and III (Cambridge, 1980, 1984), *Bach, Handel, Scarlatti 1685–1985* (Cambridge, 1985), *Perspectives on Mozart Performance* with R. Larry Todd (Cambridge, 1991) and *The Organ in Western Culture 750–1250* (Cambridge, 1993).

# CAMBRIDGE MUSIC HANDBOOKS

GENERAL EDITOR Julian Rushton

*Recent titles*

Bach: *The Brandenburg Concertos* MALCOLM BOYD
Bartók: *Concerto for Orchestra* DAVID COOPER
The Beatles: *Sgt. Pepper's Lonely Hearts Club Band* ALLAN MOORE
Beethoven: *Eroica Symphony* THOMAS SIPE
Beethoven: *Pastoral Symphony* DAVID WYN JONES
Beethoven: The 'Moonlight' and other Sonatas, Op. 27
and Op. 31 TIMOTHY JONES
Beethoven: Symphony No. 9 NICHOLAS COOK
Beethoven: Violin Concerto ROBIN STOWELL
Berlioz: *Roméo et Juliette* JULIAN RUSHTON
Brahms: Clarinet Quintet COLIN LAWSON
Brahms: *A German Requiem* MICHAEL MUSGRAVE
Brahms: Symphony No. 1 DAVID BRODBECK
Britten: *War Requiem* MERVYN COOKE
Bruckner: Symphony No. 8 BENJAMIN M. KORSTVEDT
Chopin: The Piano Concertos JOHN RINK
Debussy: *La mer* SIMON TREZISE
Dowland: Lachrimae (1604) PETER HOLMAN
Dvořák: Cello Concerto JAN SMACZNY
Elgar: *'Enigma' Variations* JULIAN RUSHTON
Gershwin: *Rhapsody in Blue* DAVID SCHIFF
Haydn: The 'Paris' Symphonies BERNARD HARRISON
Haydn: String Quartets, Op. 50 W. DEAN SUTCLIFFE
Holst: *The Planets* RICHARD GREENE
Ives: *Concord Sonata* GEOFFREY BLOCK
Liszt: Sonata in B Minor KENNETH HAMILTON
Mahler: *Das Lied von der Erde* STEPHEN E. HEFLING
Mahler: Symphony No. 3 PETER FRANKLIN
Mendelssohn: *The Hebrides* and other overtures R. LARRY TODD
Messiaen: *Quatuor pour la fin du temps* ANTHONY POPLE
Monteverdi: Vespers (1610) JOHN WHENHAM
Mozart: Clarinet Concerto COLIN LAWSON
Mozart: The 'Haydn' Quartets JOHN IRVING
Mozart: The 'Jupiter' Symphony ELAINE R. SISMAN
Mozart: Piano Concertos Nos. 20 and 21 DAVIS GRAYSON
Nielsen: Symphony No. 5 DAVID FANNING
Sibelius: Symphony No. 5 JAMES HEPOKOSKI
Strauss: *Also sprach Zarathustra* JOHN WILLIAMSON
Stravinsky: *The Rite of Spring* PETER HILL
Tippett: *A Child of our Time* KENNETH GLOAG
Verdi: Requiem DAVID ROSEN
Vivaldi: *The Four Seasons* and other concertos, Op. 8 PAUL EVERETT

*Bach: The Goldberg Variations*

*Peter Williams*

PUBLISHED BY THE PRESS SYNDICATE OF THE UNIVERSITY OF CAMBRIDGE
The Pitt Building, Trumpington Street, Cambridge, United Kingdom

CAMBRIDGE UNIVERSITY PRESS
The Edinburgh Building, Cambridge CB2 2RU, UK
40 West 20th Street, New York, NY 10011-4211, USA
10 Stamford Road, Oakleigh, VIC 3166, Australia
Ruiz de Alarcón 13, 28014 Madrid, Spain
Dock House, The Waterfront, Cape Town 8001, South Africa

http://www.cambridge.org

First published 2001

Printed in the United Kingdom at the University Press, Cambridge

*Typeface* EhrhardtMT 10.5/13 pt.     *System* LATEX 2$_\varepsilon$   [TB]

*A catalogue record for this book is available from the British Library.*

*Library of Congress Cataloguing in Publication data*
Williams, Peter F.
Bach: the Goldberg variations / Peter Williams. – 1st ed.
p.   cm.
Includes bibliographical references (p.) and index.
ISBN 0 521 80735 2 (hardback) – ISBN 0 521 00193 5 (paperback)
1. Bach, Johann Sebastian, 1685–1750. Goldberg-Variationen.   I. Title.
MT145.B14 W55 2001
786.4′1825 – dc21   2001025616

ISBN 0 521 80735 2 hardback
ISBN 0 521 00193 5 paperback

# Contents

# Abbreviations

BG      *J. S. Bachs Werke. Gesamtausgabe der Bachgesellschaft* (Leipzig: Breitkopf & Härtel, 1851–99)

BWV      Wolfgang Schmieder, *Thematisch-systematisches Verzeichnis der musikalischen Werke von Johann Sebastian Bach. Bach-Werke-Verzeichnis. 2. überarbeitete und erweiterte Ausgabe* (Wiesbaden: Breitkopf & Härtel, 1990)

Dok II      ed. Werner Neumann and Hans-Joachim Schulze, *Fremdschriftliche und gedruckte Dokumente zur Lebensgeschichte Johann Sebastian Bachs. Bach-Dokumente Bd II* (Kassel/Leipzig: Bärenreiter/DVfM, 1969)

Dok III      ed. Hans-Joachim Schulze, *Dokumente zum Nachwirken Johann Sebastian Bachs 1750–1800. Bach-Dokumente Bd III* (Kassel/Leipzig: Bärenreiter/DVfM, 1972)

KB      *Johann Sebastian Bach Neue Ausgabe sämtlicher Werke* vol. V/2 (1981), *Kritischer Bericht*, ed. Walter Emery and Christoph Wolff

NBA      *Neue Bach-Ausgabe. Johann Sebastian Bach. Neue Ausgabe sämtlicher Werke. Herausgegeben vom Johann-Sebastian-Bach-Institut Göttingen und vom Bach-Archiv Leipzig* (Leipzig/Kassel: DVfM/Bärenreiter, 1954–)

Obituary      Dok III, especially p. 85

# Introduction

## The hallowed reputation

When in 1935 the American harpsichordist Ralph Kirkpatrick prefaced his playing edition of the *Goldberg Variations* with a quote from Sir Thomas Browne's *Religio medici* of 1642 – 'there is something in it of Divinity more than the eare discovers' – he was not meaning to use it as an example of English aesthetics of the late Renaissance and platonic ideals of soundless music. Rather, he was looking for a way to signal his own admiration and enthusiasm for a unique piece of actual music, to invoke not so much the cleverness of its strategy and tactics as the kind of spiritual world it seems to occupy and the special feelings it arouses in both player and listener. To listen to or play any of the *Goldberg Variations* seems to many people more than a 'merely musical' experience, and its appearance in modern recital programmes attracts special attention as a peak to be scaled by the harpsichordist or a work to approach with respect by the pianist. I think myself that it 'feels special' because, whatever antecedent this or that feature has, its beauty is both original – seldom like anything else, even in Bach – and at the same time comprehensible, intelligible, coherent, based on simple, 'truthful' harmonies. The *Goldberg* has its own language, but one made from standard vocabulary.

The uniqueness of this music can be expressed in a more mundane way, for example by describing it as 'the largest single keyboard composition published at any time during the eighteenth century'. Or historians trying to place it might point out how often a set of variations does indeed represent a period's keyboard music at its best: Byrd's *Walsingham*, Frescobaldi's *Cento partite*, Beethoven's *Diabelli* or late sonatas, Brahms's or Rakhmaninov's *Paganini*. The awe the *Goldberg* inspires in musicians might take the form of admiration (of an apparently objective kind) for the effortless way the variations adopt virtually any up-to-date musical genre of the time. Or its emotional impact on later composers can be illustrated by finding similarities between, say, its Variation 25 and Beethoven's *Diabelli Variations* No. 31. Or some modern listeners, less willing now to speak in Romantic terms, tend to cloak their admiration for the *Goldberg* by erecting intricate schemes of symbolism or rhetoric around it, enthusiastically proving the work to be based on (to take two instances) Renaissance cosmology or Roman oratory.

But like any great piece of music, what the *Goldberg* really brings to the listener is a world of experience otherwise unknown, and I am not sure anyone can succeed in describing that world to others. What kind of language could convey the realm of the imagination opened up by its very opening bar? Or the feelings aroused by the final dying away of the theme, after it has returned and been heard the second time? This repeat of the Aria seems itself to say something about the strange power of great music, for as one hears it a final time, its aura is different. It has changed from a greeting to a farewell, from elegantly promising to sadly concluding. But how can that be, when the notes are the same and even the manner of playing them need not have changed?

Well before the nineteenth-century editions of the *Goldberg* – the first to appear after the original print of 1741 – admiration for it had spread beyond the borders of Saxony, or so one can suppose from an unusually lengthy extract in Sir John Hawkins's *History of Music* (London, 1776), which gives the Aria plus Variations Nos. 9 and 10 complete, though without commentary. Evidently Hawkins knew these movements not, as one might suppose, from a copy given him by the composer's youngest son (Johann Christian), then living in London, but from a manuscript apparently given by Sebastian himself to an English visitor to Leipzig in 1749 (probably one James Hutton, a Moravian – see Dok III, p. 311). In such ways the work was already being 'used' by authors: while Hawkins gathered such musical examples as other English gentlemen of the time collected orchids or beetles, biographers of the German Enlightenment period used such complex musical works for the ideal picture of the self-taught, hard-working, stay-at-home German genius. Bach's Obituary already had several anecdotes of the kind useful for such pictures, including the famous account of the *Goldberg* as a cure for insomnia.

But admiration for the ingenuities of the *Goldberg* might deflect one from its more elusive qualities: the special tone of it, so distinct that once initiated one is unlikely, I think, to mistake it for any other work, even in the shortest of extracts. A more modern way to express mysterious beauty than Thomas Browne's word 'divinity' is Harold Bloom's word 'uncanny': that mysterious property of the *Goldberg* as we are transported to a world of unfamiliar but not obscure sound, something inexpressible and puzzling. The historian can make prosaic points about, say, the final return of the theme, pointing out that another publication had done this recently (see below, p. 92) and that it actually produces a shape very suitable for new kinds of public recital. But to any listener, its eventual dying away is one of music's most touching moments.

## The popular name '*Goldberg*'

The list of printed works in Bach's Obituary, eventually published in 1754, speaks of 'An Aria with 30 Variations, for two *Claviere*' or manuals, which is partly but not exactly quoting the original title page appearing early in the deceased's final decade:

> Clavier Ubung bestehend in einer Aria mit verschiedenen Veraenderungen vors Clavicimbal mit 2 Manualen

> Keyboard Practice, consisting of an Aria with diverse variations for the harpsichord with 2 manuals

The title goes on to express a formal purpose virtually identical to that of three other books of 'Keyboard Practice' previously published (Books I, II and III described below): it was a work

> denen Liebhabern zur Gemüths-Ergetzung verfertiget

> prepared for the soul's delight of music-lovers.

Other translations for the phrase 'soul's delight' can, like this one, easily miss the pious connotations it had for the orthodox Lutheran believer. For him, spirits are refreshed or re-created not merely for idle pleasure but to prepare us for further work in the talents that have been entrusted to us, and this for the sake of our neighbour. Much more than an empty formula, the phrase suggests that any such volume of music was not to be taken as the vainglorious product of some showy performer but was, indeed, a pious offering. Something similar had appeared on the title page of a publication in Leipzig by one of the town's previous organists, Daniel Vetter of St Nicholas's.[1]

More interesting than such formulas to a later German biographer like J. N. Forkel, author in 1802 of the first major Bach monograph, were personal stories and heart-warming anecdotes. Although in Chapter 6 he refers to the *Goldberg* only as 'the great variations' ('den grossen Variationen', p. 31), in a later chapter he writes more about it than about any other work of Bach but the *Art of Fugue*, which he takes to be the final opus. (This work too, by the way, offered an intriguing combination of contrapuntally clever music and touchingly personal anecdote – in this case, a story concerning the so-called *Deathbed Chorale* and the sad fact or supposed fact that the composer had died before completing the most complex movement of the work as a whole.) Presumably on the basis of what he had learnt from correspondence with the Bach sons Philipp Emanuel Bach or (more likely) Wilhelm Friedemann, Forkel tells the following well-known story about the *Goldberg* and how it came about.

It seems that in Dresden at the time, the influential Count Keyserlingk (the courtier Hermann Carl, Reichsgraf von Keyserlingk, with whom Bach stayed in November 1741), employed a young house-musician, Johann Gottlieb Goldberg. The Count

> kränkelte viel und hatte dann schlaflose Nächte. Goldberg ... musste in solchen Zeiten in einem Nebenzimmer die Nacht zubringen, um ihm während der Schlaflosigkeit etwas vorzuspielen. Einst äusserte der Graf gegen Bach, dass er gern einige Clavierstücke für seinen Goldberg haben möchte, die so sanften und etwas muntern Charakters wären, dass er dadurch in seinen schlaflosen Nächten ein wenig aufgeheitert werden könnte. Bach glaubte, diesen Wunsch am besten durch Variationen erfüllen zu können, die er bisher, der stets gleichen Grundharmonie wegen, für eine undankbare Arbeit gehalten hatte. (Forkel, *Bach*, pp. 51–2)

was often unwell and then had sleepless nights. On these occasions, Goldberg had to spend the night in an adjoining room so that he could play something to him during this sleeplessness. The Count once remarked in Bach's presence that he would very much like to have some keyboard pieces for his Goldberg, of a character so gentle and somewhat merry that he could be a little cheered up by them in his sleepless nights. Bach believed that he could best fulfil this wish with some variations, which until then he had held to be a thankless task because of the basic harmony always being the same.

But no dedication to the Count is documented on the title page or any known copy, and while this is not conclusive, the likely period of composition (about 1739–40) hardly fits in with the age and putative abilities of young Goldberg, who was born in 1727. The likeliest explanation is that when J. S. Bach made that particular visit to Dresden in 1741, perhaps not least to see his beloved son Wilhelm Friedemann, he brought with him, and at some point presented to the Count, a signed copy of the set of variations newly engraved in Nuremberg and now on sale. Not unlikely is that the whole incident was first set in motion, then witnessed and finally narrated to Forkel (having been embroidered over time, perhaps) by Wilhelm Friedemann. Note that only in the last clause does Forkel imply that the variations would not have been composed except in this connection, something he could have misunderstood when the tale was told him – the rest could be taken to mean that having some variations to hand, Bach thought them suitable for the Count's need when he came to hear of it. (Chronology can easily become elided, just as it was when a chorale first said to have been 'dictated by Bach in his blindness' later became one 'dictated on his deathbed'.)

Either way, we could speculate further and suppose that the virtuoso in the mind of the composer as he produced these demanding pieces was not young Goldberg or even himself but Wilhelm Friedemann: it was for him that Sebastian had already assembled several volumes of music (the *Clavierbüchlein*, the Six Sonatas for organ, and perhaps Book 1 of the *Well-tempered Clavier*) and probably fair-copied another masterpiece for his first professional audition (the 'Great' Praeludium in G major, for the job of organist in the prestigious Sophienkirche, Dresden, in 1733).[2] Not impossible too is that in some sense it was for Friedemann that Sebastian had planned, composed and published all three previous volumes of 'Keyboard Practice', and later was moved to transcribe – or allow someone to transcribe – the *Schübler Chorales* for organ, including the well-known setting 'Wachet auf!' (These chorales Friedemann doubtless played when he became the newly appointed organist at the Liebfrauenkirche, Halle, about that time.)³ There is no document now linking any of these works with Friedemann, except that he had copies of the *Schübler Chorales* for sale. But that the father supplied the son with virtuoso pieces with which to make a stir as a harpsichordist in a cosmopolitan capital city, and as organist in one of its churches, is more than possible.

Two further details in Forkel's story raise questions about his reliability in musical matters. First, his phrase 'gentle and somewhat merry' hardly conveys the impression left by the *Goldberg Variations*. Did a composer expect players to pick and choose which variations to play, or was it that Forkel's respect got in the way of grasping the impression the work makes in practice? Or – and this is to put greater trust in Forkel – is the brilliance of modern performances an anachronism, and are the variations more gentle than we now think? Secondly, while it seems the case that after youthful attempts at keyboard variations (including the so-called Chorale Partitas) Bach did shun them in the form familiar to so many of his contemporaries, a 'thankless task' is hardly the way to view other masterpieces of his in the field of harmonic variations, the Chaconne in D minor for violin and the Passacaglia in C minor for organ. Forkel knew these pieces but appears not to have seen – as Bach himself surely saw – that they have important points in common with the *Goldberg*.

Looking at these three pieces now, we can recognize them as presenting three commanding conceptions of variation form, unmatched as a group in the work of any other composer, each totally different in strategy and tactics, but all of them obviously aiming to wrest harmonic variety and create substantial works by deferring to (not merely decorating) a pattern of chords – a pattern moreover which is in itself already coherent, convincing, logical and, above all, potentially melodious. It would have been a 'thankless task' to write the usual kind of variations in which a melody and its (simple) harmonies were decorated with standard note-patterns, and no mature sets of variations by J. S. Bach are of this kind.

## The formal name '*Clavierübung IV*'

For convenience, this Handbook will continue to refer to the Variations for Harpsichord in G major, BWV 988, as the *Goldberg*, aware that in much German scholarship the name *Klavierübung IV* is often used. Here too, however, the received title is not quite straightforward.

Although neither the volume's original title page nor the Obituary calls it 'Part IV' of 'Keyboard Practice', the custom of doing so was established once and for all in 1853 when the Bach Society edition (BG vol. III) grouped it with the three previous volumes of harpsichord and organ music called *Clavierübung*. (These are described briefly in Chapter 1, below.) Publishing the four as a single volume in this way implied something more than when an individual owner of a *Goldberg* copy happened to mark it 'Part IV' by hand, as must have been the case now and then (for an example, see KB, p. 103); but the power of a monumental nineteenth-century edition to imply this 'something more' might not be justified. The original ornate and elegant title page was quite different from that of the three earlier volumes, and up to that point all Bach's published keyboard music had been called *Clavierübung*.

Thus, why the volume was not officially called 'Part IV' or 'Opus IV' raises several questions, such as whether yet later volumes also belonged in some sense to the series. It is true that following custom, the *Goldberg* publisher, Balthasar Schmid of Nuremberg, was unlikely to acknowledge in this way a series he himself had not previously published; *his* was not a fourth part of anything. But he had also been involved in Parts II and III and some years later was to publish the *Canonic Variations* for organ, which would then have been 'Part V' or even 'Part VI', had they or any further publication (such as the set of chorales called *Schübler*) still kept the general title of 'Keyboard Practice'. But this was becoming an archaic term.

In any case, finding titles seems not to have been a prime consideration for J. S. Bach. Some major keyboard compilations – the original *Orgelbüchlein*, the Six Sonatas for organ, the so-called *Well-tempered Clavier* Book 2, the late collection of organ chorales (nicknamed 'The Eighteen') and even the *Art of Fugue* – received no final title or title page. If any or all of these were or came to be intended for publication, as they might well have been during the new market-expansion of the 1740s, there is always a faint possibility that they too could have kept the generic title of 'Keyboard Practice Part X, consisting of...'. To see only the *Goldberg Variations* as part of some intended grand sequence, therefore, may well reflect the influence of the nineteenth-century Complete

Edition on subsequent references and editions, including the titles and terminology in the *New Bach Edition* and the BWV catalogue, which always speak of *Klavierübung IV*.

Nevertheless, for present purposes, and so long as other collections like the *Art of Fugue* are borne in mind, there are good reasons for taking the four volumes of *Clavierübung* in sequence as we have them, for each, in its way, is a highly organized and explicit collection of musical techniques, theoretical allusion and practical usefulness. Furthermore, some looking back might be discernible in each successive volume, though to recognize this could lead to exaggeration and encourage fanciful speculation, especially the kind involving number-counting. However all this might be, Chapter 1 surveys these previous collections of 'Keyboard Practice' in the belief that with them some idea can be glimpsed of the composer's original conception and its part in the compendium of musical techniques he seems to have spent so much of his life assembling.

## A note on editions

The Bach Society edition of 1853 (BG vol. III, ed. C. F. Becker) is based on one example of the first print but has no critical commentary; its Dover reprint of 1970 unfortunately reduces the page-size. Kirkpatrick's edition referred to above (Schirmer 1935, with reprints) has a lengthy preface raising many questions of interpretation and performance, not without anachronism but still useful for study by performers. The Peters edition by Kurt Soldan (EP 4462, originally 1937) and the Henle edition of Rudolf Steglich (originally 1962) use one or two manuscript sources as well as a first print, but by far the most authoritative is the *Neue Bach-Ausgabe* vol. V/2 (Christoph Wolff, 1977) and its Critical Commentary of 1981 (KB or *Kritischer Bericht*, pp. 91–143, 153–5). Though not without begging some questions, this draws for its text on the so-called 'composer's copy' of the print, the rediscovery of which in France was announced by Olivier Alain in 1975. This has a few autograph markings and/or corrections, plus – most significantly – the 'Fourteen Canons', BWV 1087, an autograph manuscript copy of pieces otherwise unknown as a set (see below).

This 'composer's copy' is also the source for an inexpensive and 'cleaned up' facsimile edition published in 1990 by Editions Fuzeau (No. 2811), with introduction by Philippe Lescat. Apart from some notation in the tenor clef from time to time, this or any facsimile edi-tion need not give much trouble to a player already somewhat acquainted with the work, and it is warmly recommended. Of course a facsim-ile conveys such detail as the symmetrical pagination described below, though the consequence of this is a (superficially) cramped appearance, despite some slight enlargement in the Fuzeau reproduction. A more evocative and elegant facsimile is published by Peters (1984), based on another copy of the print, and completed by a booklet in which the editor, Christoph Wolff, describes all four *Clavierübung* volumes in facsimile, their history, publication process and various other matters arising.

## The intended harpsichord

As with the organ works of J. S. Bach, the question 'What kind of instru-ment is most appropriate to this music?' is complex and needs careful wording. There seem to be several kinds of question:

What range of instrument-types was familiar at the period and could have been in the mind of the composer, or owned by any of his buyers?

What was the average or normal instrument of the time and place, and does this music have special requirements beyond it?

What is lost if an instrument of another type, including modern harp-sichords or even other keyboard instruments, is used instead?

The following remarks are concerned with the second of these questions, for the other two pass into realms involving far more than the *Goldberg Variations*. The first question requires a lengthy description of many instrument-types made in a country whose first keyboard-love was the or-gan and whose harpsichords are either simple work-horses or extravagant pseudo-organs with many sets of strings – individual or unique artefacts following no regular model. The third requires a probing of aesthetic issues that arise when music is transcribed (as when a modern piano is used for the *Goldberg*) or original timbres are imitated (as when a modern harpsichord copy is used) and is not unique to this repertory. However, these are the issues raised in any modern performance of the work, and an answer to the second question might point in a helpful direction.

Few technical details are known about the harpsichords in J. S. Bach's possession at any period of his life or how exclusive he was in his tastes and preferences, but the following states the background to the *Goldberg*:

Although two manuals are not absolutely necessary to play all the notes, they are specified on the title page, obligatory for eleven variations and optional for three others.

The compass required is GG–d''' (Philipp Emanuel's Sonatas of 1742 require top e'''').

The normal difference in tone between two rows of unison strings allows both parity in the two-part dialogues and a solo line for the right hand of Variations 13 and 25 (there are no left-hand solos as found in some organ works). This tone-difference will usually, perhaps always, mean that the right hand plays on the lower manual, the left on the upper.

The period concerned is *c.* 1735–40.

The music seems to have various links with Dresden.

No particular effects or 'registrations' are specified.

It could be that the composer has consciously used the top and bottom notes normally available, as was certainly the case in some of his organ music. Such an overall compass was also required for *Clavierübung I*, while that for *Clavierübung II* was yet shorter (AA–c''').[4] By 1740, these were old-fashioned compasses, but perhaps that was deliberate: they not only allowed older instruments to play the work but all things being equal, a longer compass (including that of most harpsichords made today) helps produce a different tone and encourages a colouristic approach to music rather alien to the counterpoint of the *Goldberg*. There is another advantage with a 'minimum instrument': it need have no 4' row of strings influencing the behaviour of the soundboard, or any colour stop (lute, harp etc.) influencing the behaviour of the player. The four extant harpsichords by Michael Mietke, one of whose instruments was bought for Köthen in 1719 and collected in Berlin by J. S. Bach, have a compass only to c''', d''' (2) or e'''.

On the other hand, larger instruments, perhaps with more than three sets of strings, a longer compass and some 'colours' (suboctave strings, lute or harp effects, nasal tone on the upper manual, three sets of 8′ strings) were known at the period, so much so that Philipp Emanuel included registrations or suggestions for stop-changes in a set of variations he originally composed in 1747 (W 69). One assumes that as with organ music, performers made use of whatever potential for colour their instruments had, i.e. two manuals were optional not obligatory. In this respect, the many large or extravagant harpsichords mentioned in various German sources of the time are no more and no less relevant to the *Goldberg* than Silbermann's biggest organs are to the Prelude and Fugue in E♭ from *Clavierübung III*. The *Goldberg* itself is not written in such a way as to require an instrument to have even the kind of rich or colourful tone in the tenor and bass that is essential for the French repertory.

An instrument of *c.* 1740 currently in Dresden (Schloss Pillnitz), and attributed to the Court builder J. H. Gräbner, has a specification of the kind common throughout northern Europe by the 1740s, typical of instruments on which buyers of the *Goldberg* may have played it. There are two manuals FF–f‴ and three rows of strings. It is also veneered, unusually for the period and place but recalling one of the instruments listed in the inventory made on J. S. Bach's death (Dok II, p. 492). Also trustworthy as a standard two-manual model might be the Dresden harpsichord of 1774 by J. H. Gräbner the Younger, now in the Musikinstrumenten-Museum of the University of Leipzig and typical of the work of a family of Court instrument-makers contributing to Dresden's active musical life during the *Goldberg*'s period:

two manuals, FF–f‴

three rows (8′, 4′, 8′), a lute-stop (buff) on the upper manual

probably brass strings

no coupler but upper 8′ available on lower manual through dogleg

hand stops above upper manual, left and right on the nameboard

Construction is lighter, and the string-scaling shorter, than is the case with the bigger Hamburg harpsichord-types or those of contemporary England. The tone is unlikely to have been as bright and resonant as that of most modern instruments, or of those built both then and now in the French taste. But the more neutral tone would have expressed the counterpoint appropriately, as too in their way might that of the new and discreet-sounding fortepianos being made in the years around 1740 by Gottfried Silbermann, in nearby Freiberg, Saxony.

Plates 1a & 1b. Two-manual harpsichord by Johann Heinrich Gräbner, Dresden 1774. Musikinstrumenten-Museum der Universität Leipzig, Inv.-Nr. 91. Reproduced by permission of the Museum

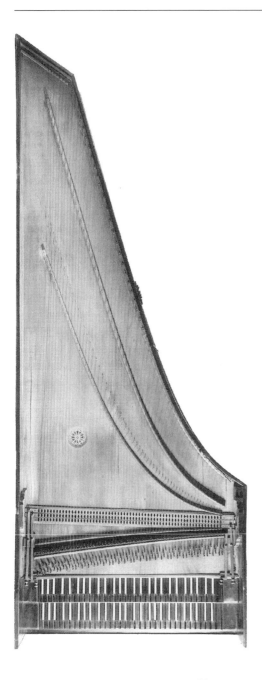

# 1

## *Background and genesis*

### *Clavierübung*

Quite what the implications of the curiously unprepossessing term 'Keyboard Practice' are is less clear than one might suppose. Players now are used to Studies or *études*, Exercises or *essercizi*, and every child knows that 'to practise' means 'to exercise oneself in the performance of music with the view of acquiring skill' (OED). Clearly, with the *Goldberg Variations* one does do this, and an English publisher of the time might well have called them *Lessons for the Harpsichord*, when 'lesson' suggested written-down music helpful to players, either as practical instruction or as substitutes for compositions and improvisations of their own. But there is another kind of practice, the kind spoken of by lawyers and doctors as they 'practise a profession' or 'put their subject into practice' or even 'buy into a practice': this is practice as distinct from theory.

*Musica prattica* had been a common term in treatises of sixteenth- and seventeenth-century Italy and in those elsewhere imitating or influenced by them, treatises applying the rules of harmony and counterpoint for the creating of actual, written-down music. When in 1689 Johann Kuhnau – uncommonly for the time, a university graduate (Leipzig, in law) and not averse to literary conceits – came to publish a set of seven harpsichord suites in his university town, he seems to have coined the term *Clavier-Übung* as a German equivalent of the venerable Italian term. After all, the volume would instruct the buyer not only in keyboard dexterity but in the practical application of musical theory, in so far as each suite gave an example of the major keys (C, D, E, F, G, A and B♭) rather than the old modes or tones, and recognized the seven notes of the scale (rather than the six of ancient hexachordal theory) as the basis of harmony as currently understood and applied. A further set of seven suites followed in 1692, now in the minor (C, D, E, F, G, A, B), the two books thus 'fixing' the idea of the diatonic keys, the majors and minors. Kuhnau's music itself may not rank with the suites of older German composers like Buxtehude or, much less, Froberger, but in its way was instructive and usefully up to date.

Some other composers older than Bach used the term *Clavier-Übung*, notably Johann Krieger in 1698 (Nuremberg) and Johann Christoph Bach in 1709 (the 'Gehren cantor' Bach, in a manuscript compilation). Although these and perhaps others were probably following Kuhnau, one can suppose that when the term was used in later publications – by Vincent Lübeck in 1728 (Hamburg), G. A. Sorge in 1739 (Nuremberg), J. C. Graupner (Darmstadt *c.* 1730) and J. L. Krebs (three parts, Nuremberg) – it was J. S. Bach who was the inspiration. From Krieger on, the term could have been understood to cover a wide variety of music for a wide variety of keyboard instruments, and it is possible that Bach too used it with a long-term plan in mind to survey as many as he could of the more elevated genres of keyboard music. But only suppositions can be made from his volumes, none of which, rather surprisingly for the time, contained a preface of any kind.

When he turned to publishing his first keyboard works, Bach began with only one, the Partita in B♭, 1726, promising others in an advertisement. This work might be seen as picking up with the key on which Kuhnau's first series had ended, and one might not be far wrong in supposing that with it Bach was saluting his predecessor, even establishing the right of apostolic succession to him in Leipzig, and achieving it with – would it not have been obvious? – very superior music. Kuhnau had died in 1722, and Bach eventually succeeded him as cantor of St Thomas, having long been familiar with his music and collaborating with him on some major organ-building projects.

## *Clavierübung I*

So 'Keyboard Practice' was initiated in 1726 with a single suite, described in an advertisement as 'the first partita' of 'a collection of clavier suites' (Dok II, pp. 160–1).

The Italian term *partita* had been used by Krieger on a bilingual title page of 1697 as an equivalent to the German term *Partie* (*Sechs*

*Musicalische Partien/ Sei partite musicali*), and Bach too seems to use it in the sense of 'a part' or 'a division' of a whole, specifically of a volume called 'Keyboard Practice'. As such, whatever dictionaries now say, *partita* does not mean *suite* without further qualification. In *partien* Kuhnau seems again to have coined a word, taken up by his Leipzig pupil J. C. Graupner (*Partien*, 1718); its singular in Italian Bach had taken to be *Partia* when he compiled his three suites for solo violin. Neither Kuhnau nor Bach had the much earlier Italian term *partita* in mind, for *partite* were variations not suites, indeed an equivalent to the old English word 'divisions' for a set of variations. Despite the usual assumptions now made, whether Bach himself ever used the word *partita* either for his sets of chorale-variations for organ (the so-called Chorale Partitas) or for his suites for solo violin (the so-called Violin Partitas) is not certain.

Harpsichord Partitas 2, 3, 4, 5 and 6 followed in 1727, 1727, 1728, 1730 and 1730/1, and in 1731 the six were gathered together as a set and published. Note that while the individual suites had been published as *Clavierübung . . . Partita 1* [*etc.*], the composite title says nothing about partitas:

> Clavir Ubung bestehend in Praeludien, Allemanden, Couranten, Saraban-den, Giguen, Menuetten, und andern Galanterien; Denen Liebhabern zur Gemüths Ergoetzung verfertiget von Johann Sebastian Bach. Hochfürstl: Sächsisch-Weisenfelsischen würcklichen Capellmeistern und Directore Chori Musici Lipsiensis. Opus I. In Verlegung des Autoris. 1731

> Keyboard practice consisting of Preludes, Allemandes, Courantes, Sara-bandes, Gigues, Minuets and other *galanteries*. Prepared for the soul's delight of music-lovers by Johann Sebastian Bach, at present capell-meister to His Highness the Prince of Saxe-Weissenfels and Director of the Choristers, Leipzig. Opus I. Published by the author. 1731

One of the two engravers, music students working for a Leipzig printer (see account in Butler, 'The Engraving'), was much more skilled than the other.

The sequence of keys is more complex and symmetrical than Kuhnau's, or of course Bach's own step-by-step sequence in the *Well-tempered Clavier* of 1722, and produces a wedge-like pattern of tonics:

B♭ major, C minor, A minor, D major, G major, E minor

No French books of harpsichord music had their keys as systematically planned as this, nor for such secular music did they follow the order of church tones (I, II, III = D minor, G minor, A minor, etc.), as they often did in the *Livres d'orgue*. Each partita has seven movements except for No. 2, though this could also be counted as having seven (the long opening movement of No. 2 has a slow section, unlike the prelude and fugue found in two other partitas). Six movements from each of Nos. 3 and 6 had appeared as suites in the *Anna Magdalena Book* of 1725, made there evidently from a yet earlier copy and left without title.[1] I do not know exactly where Bach's term *Galanterien* for the less formal suite-dances came from, but this or a cognate tends to occur when theorists (such as Brossard in 1703 or Mattheson in 1739) described or categorized the varieties of musical styles, high and low.

Variety is certainly an aim of *Clavierübung Opus I*, but within the tight confines of a conventional and narrow genre. While no two Allemandes or Courantes or Sarabandes or Gigues in the set of six are quite alike, they could not be anything else. My impression is that no two even have the same tempo. Such an approach produces not only strikingly original conceptions (e.g. the Correntes in Nos. 1 and 3) but movements in which familiar conventions take on a wonderfully idealized form (e.g. the French Courantes in Nos. 2 and 4, the Italian Correntes in Nos. 5 and 6). Like Kuhnau's *Partien*, each begins with a prelude, and each prelude is distinct in genre, form, style, texture and even in name. The different titles, some of them less than obviously appropriate (Sinfonia in Partita No. 2, Fantasia in No. 3, Praeambulum in No. 5), recall Johann Mattheson's in his *Pièces de clavecin* (London, 1714), not least as the opening movements of Nos. 3 and 6 had been called merely *Prélude* in their earlier versions. Though far from being great or even at times competent pieces, Mattheson's had been the last notable German publication of suites, except for Handel's so-called *Eight Great Suites* (London, 1719/20), which too had rung the changes rather less systematically. In addition to the Six Partitas' incomparable quality, it is their *systematic* variety that is so striking and of course typical of all four volumes of *Clavierübung*, each of which has its own *system*.

A major challenge is to find likely influences behind the Six Partitas, for however original and sophisticated, J. S. Bach was a composer who knew, thought about and reacted to a great deal of music, far more than documents reveal. Was he familiar with such recent books as Handel's of 1719/20, Couperin's *Troisième Livre* of 1722 and, in particular, Rameau's *Pièces de clavecin* of 1724? Take one striking detail: eight of Couperin's fifty-four movements in the book of 1722 are in 2/4 time, the new Italian metre which had not yet appeared in any of Bach's suite-compilations, for keyboard, for violin or for cello.[2] But the Six Partitas now include three examples of this metre, all with Italian titles of questionable aptness – Capriccio, Scherzo, Aria – and it must remain possible that Couperin's book was treated as a guide to modern tastes, as indeed it deserves to be. In the same connection, it is significant that there had been no 2/4 Scherzo in the early version of the A minor Partita; and its Burlesca, which was first called Menuet, perhaps owed its name-change to the unusual rubric used by Couperin for one of the pieces in his *Troisième Livre*: 'dans le goût burlesque'.

One also needs to bear in mind less major composers, such as J. G. Graun (violin teacher of Wilhelm Friedemann in the mid-1720s), whose sonatas published in *c.* 1726 include many movements in 2/4 time. Also, the farther back any apparent allusion or imitation goes – for example, the Gigue of No. 3 seems to develop a fugue-type found in a sonata of Adam Reinken, 1687, transcribed by Bach (BWV 965) – the likelier that it would be updated or somehow built upon for the new publication. Or the poorer the influential music, the more it would be re-conceived: the wonderfully high seriousness and harmonic tension of No. 2's opening Sinfonia might be a creative response to the puny *Symphonie* of Mattheson's Suite No. 10. So might the unique Capriccio of No. 2 be to the violinistic figures in sonatas by J. G. Graun. Various galant touches in No. 5, the most modern of the partitas, might also be imaginative reactions to near-banalities in Graun's modishly galant opus. Nor should one forget that Bach must always have had his own music in mind: one can see the Air in Partita No. 6 or even the startlingly original Corrente of No. 1 as maturer versions of movements in the recent French Suites for harpsichord. Even the relentless Gigue of the E minor Partita, a source in modern times for much speculation on jigged rhythms in general and circle time-signatures in particular, could well be viewed as an 'extended' version of the simpler Gigue of the French Suite in D minor.

Rameau's second book of *Pièces de clavecin* (1724) was without rival at the time for both its musical and its didactic qualities, and while there is no documented evidence that J. S. Bach knew it, nor is there that he had once known the organ volumes of Louis Marchand and André Raison from which he seems to have borrowed themes. Is it not possible that, to take one example, the unique Gigue of the B♭ major Partita is responding to Rameau's remarks about hand-crossing in which

> la main gauche passe pardessus la droite, pour toucher alternativement la Basse & le Dessus. Je crois que ces dernieres batteries me sont particulieres, du moins il n'en a point encore paru de la sorte; & je puis dire en leur faveur que l'œil y partage le plaisir qu'en reçoit l'oreille.

> the left hand passes above the right, to play bass and treble in alternation. I think that these latter *batteries* are particular to myself, at least nothing of the kind has yet appeared in print, and I can say in their favour that the eye shares in the pleasure that the ear has of them.

– the last remark surely striking a chord with Bach? In the case of No. 5, there is a further possible connection. Published in 1730, it must have been the last to be composed, musically the most modern of the six. But by then, Rameau's newer book (1728/9) had also appeared, and No. 5 shows various signs of responding – indeed, immediately responding – to these up-to-the-minute French pieces. This is a topic worth exploring elsewhere, but several details are suggestive. For example, Rameau's new book may have suggested a puzzling and unique bit of notation in Partita No. 5: the double stemming of its cross-beat Minuet, a movement of pared-down simplicity and pseudo-naivety worthy of the French master himself. One wonders whether all this was for the benefit of Wilhelm Friedemann, then nineteen or twenty years old.

I doubt if all the scope, all the levels of variety in the Six Partitas have yet been recognized. For example, one can long be familiar with No. 5 before appreciating that its movements are all in triple time, necessitating some ingenuity in the case of the Allemande, which by definition has four beats:

Praeambulum: 3/4, moderato, metre ambiguous at first

Allemande: 4/4, with triplets (so as if 24/16)

Corrente: 3/8

Sarabande: 3/4, poco andante

Tempo di Minuetta: 3/4, but simultaneously 6/8

Passepied: 3/8

Gigue: 6/8, a steadier 6/8 (so as if 2 × 3/8)

These three levels of triple time – long, short and compound – even resemble the medieval categories of mode, time and prolation, not perhaps wittingly but in so far as three levels of triple time (slow, ordinary, fast) have traditionally been recognized as having three distinct characters. Seven movements in seven different shades of triple time suggest not only deliberate planning but an intimate grasp of music's nature, as one might expect of this composer.

But in any case, the Six Partitas are not merely collections of clever ideas or, in the case of No. 6, a rather distancing thoroughness. There are also the harmonic sensuousness of the E minor Sarabande, the unending melody of the D major Allemande, the uncanny verve of the C minor fugue, the sheer charm of the B♭ Minuets, and so much else. It is striking how the very opening piece of all four volumes of 'Keyboard Practice' exposes the listener to sounds totally unknown before.

## *Clavierübung II*

An advertisement for No. 5 of *Clavierübung I* mentions two further partitas to come (Dok II, p. 202), but there was only one. So it seems that a seventh partita, presumably to match the original plan of Johann Kuhnau's *Clavier-Übung*, was never composed or completed; or it was, but it became the Ouverture in B minor, BWV 831, apparently a revised version of an Ouverture in C minor; or it was, and it turned out to be not a suite but the Italian Concerto in F major, BWV 972. Of those possibilities, the last fits the key-plan best: F major is the key next in line to *Clavierübung I*'s sequence of B♭ c a D G e. Although logically one might expect F minor to be next, those six notes themselves produce a major scale whose tonic is resoundingly confirmed with the very first chord of the Italian Concerto – in fact, the very next chord Bach published. If this is a coincidence, it is a remarkable and very musical one!

So the two works BWV 972 (Italian concerto) and 831 (French suite) constitute *Clavierübung II*, published in 1735:

Zweyter Theil der Clavier Ubung bestehend in einem Concerto nach Italiaenischen Gusto und einer Overture nach Französischer Art, vor ein Clavicymbel mit zweyen Manualen. Denen Liebhabern zur Gemüths-Ergötzung verferdiget...

Second Part of Keyboard Practice, consisting of a Concerto according to Italian taste and an Overture according to the French manner, for a harpsichord with two manuals, prepared for the soul's delight of music-lovers...

Not the least interesting detail here is the specifying of two manuals. This was not because they are necessary, as with organ trios; nor are they for the sake of a melody in long notes that has somehow to stand out, as with organ chorales; nor are they practically desirable for hand-crossing, as in the *Goldberg* (though there they are not absolutely obligatory either, as modern pianists know). Rather, two manuals are specified in order to allow *forte–piano* changes, dynamic contrasts of the kind now desired by up-to-date musicians owning one of the fashionable two-manual harpsichords, even perhaps one of the new fortepianos whose loud–soft had somehow to be imitated.

One could have played at least the preludes of the earlier Partitas 2, 4 and 6 with two manuals, but they are not specified there in *Clavierübung I* any more than they are in major organ works of the time. The same goes for a putative early version of the Italian Concerto's first movement (see below) and for Bach's earlier transcriptions for harpsichord of concertos by Vivaldi and others. In those transcriptions, the composer or a copyist might occasionally write in *f* and *p* signs to draw attention to echo passages, meanwhile leaving it also quite practical (if one did happen to have a two-manual instrument, that is) to change manuals for other reasons – such as to distinguish the *tutti* themes from the *solo* episodes typical of Italian concertos.

Sources suggest that both works in *Clavierübung II* originated some time before the print, the C minor version of the Ouverture having been copied by Anna Magdalena from an autograph score. The idea of so contrasting Italian and French styles was very much to the taste of the day amongst knowledgeable German musicians, and one finds it too with Handel. The contrast is borne out even at the end of each piece in *Clavierübung II*, for the first is marked *Il fine*, the second *Fin*. This is found in the second edition of 1736 (the first had only the *Fin*) and suggests that someone had carefully corrected it. Humour, perhaps, or pedantry? Or a merely earnest fidelity to imaginary models? Certainly the 2/4 metre of the opening movement of *Clavierübung II* was an Italian allusion, as was even the absence of a tempo-sign for it such as Allegro, since Venetian concertos too were often without one for an opening movement.[3]

In the event, however, the Italian Concerto, described by one contemporary as a perfect model of the well-designed concerto for single instrument (Dok II, p. 373), differs in major respects from actual Italian concertos of the kind that Bach had transcribed. The shape of the outer movements is more regular than Vivaldi's; in the print, the contrasts between solo *concertino* and chorus *ripieno* are explicitly scored for two manuals as never in the (much earlier) surviving transcriptions; and a strict 'Bachian' symmetry seems to be operating throughout. This last shows itself in the way the three movements seem to have been calculated and notated so as to have the same pulse: a 2/4 crotchet = a 3/4 andante quaver which = a 2/2 presto minim. In practice, this would mean playing the first movement less fast, with more deliberation, than commonly heard now. But so one ought to play a 2/4 movement. As for the idiom itself, although the *piano* solo episodes in the outer movements, and the *cantabile* melody above a *basso continuo* in the Andante, are in principle thoroughly Italianate, they are not as specifically so as, say, the opening movement of Handel's F major Suite (1719/20) for harpsichord, which is so close to Corelli in many of its details.

Nevertheless, the Italian Concerto does undeniably share some characteristics with, say, Vivaldi's Concerto in G minor as transcribed by Bach (RV 316 and BWV 975). Both the two first movements in 2/4 time, the chordal themes and passages, the running motifs and episodes, the clear *da capo* shape, even perhaps the slurs and little dactyls – all these suggest that strong impressions remained with Bach from certain music of Vivaldi learnt twenty years before *Clavierübung II* was published, as well they might, and that he wittingly alluded to them. If one compares the Vivaldi arrangement BWV 975 with Bach's Italian Concerto, it does appear likely that, though naturally with his own harmonic and melodic characteristics, Bach had picked up from Vivaldi ideas of what a concerto episode is, and how it contrasts with the main material. And yet, despite such conceptual similarities as these, nowhere does the Italian Concerto have the effortless, seemingly thoughtless, caprice of Venetian concertos, and it is unlikely ever to be mistaken for one of them. Nor vice-versa.[4]

The Ouverture in B minor, on the other hand, is very French in concept and countless stylistic details, more so than the Six Partitas or any other keyboard work of Bach since one youthful imitation (the Ouverture in F major, BWV 820). The figuration, rhythms, harmonies, textures, dance-characteristics and melodic touches are those of a composer very familiar indeed with French orchestral suites, not least from his own earlier successes in this genre. Although many details in their respective sources suggest that the C minor was the earlier version, being transposed for – and probably just before – the print, the reason for the transposition is not obvious. But it must have been compelling, since to most players the C minor version feels more idiomatic and comfortable. Of course, the Ouverture's B minor suits the published tonal scheme in so far as it is as distant as possible from the Concerto's F major. And, since both C and B minor could be seen as typically French keys for such a suite, B minor may have been simulating another French characteristic and one familiar in Dresden at the time: the taste for extra-low pitch, a semitone lower than ordinary chamber-music pitch of the time.

There is another point about the presumed transposition. One Partita in C minor was already in print, so there was no need for another. But this one, BWV 826, had been 'international', with some distinctly Italian elements (a melismatic Andante, a violinistic Fugue and Capriccio) and German ones (the Allemande). The 'newer' one, BWV 831a, was more thoroughly and consistently French, a true *ouverture* without Allemande but with a series of dances, in this respect much like Bach's so-called orchestral suites (BWV 1066–1069). Is it possible that two C minor works were conceived at much the same time and meant to be different in the styles they allude to, thus giving the composer the idea of a more complete contrast between Italian and French styles for a later publication – as in fact turned out to be the case?

## *Clavierübung III*

From the two-manual harpsichord required for *Clavierübung II*, Part III (1739) now moves to the organ:

> Dritter Theil der Clavier Übung bestehend in verschiedenen Vorspie-
> len über die Catechismus- und andere Gesaenge, vor die Orgel: Denen
> Liebhabern, und besonders denen Kennern von dergleichen Arbeit, zur
> Gemüths Ergezung verfertiget von . . .

> Third Part of Keyboard Practice, consisting of various Preludes on the
> Catechism and other hymns, for the organ; prepared for the soul's delight
> of music-lovers and especially for connoisseurs of such work by . . .[5]

The reason why the title does not ask for two manuals, as *Clavierübung II* had done, is almost certainly because organists of the time were much more used to this requirement than harpsichordists, and they would assume they needed two for at least some of the pieces in this or any collection. Had they been exceptional and fortunate enough to have three manuals at their disposal, they could certainly have found ways to use all three in the opening and closing movements, although the composer does not specify them. (The idea, born of 'purist' tendencies in the early music revival of the twentieth century, that manuals were not changed in the multi-sectional preludes and fugues of J. S. Bach and other composers is not supported by unmistakable and positive evidence, and seems against musical common sense.)

The pieces of Part III were probably being composed over the period 1735–9. Various musical stimuli can be suggested for the volume, in-cluding the wish to show how *Clavierübung II*'s French and Italian styles could be taken over and adapted to the organ. Then there was other contemporary organ music, including that of minor composers. Bach's retail agency in 1734–5 of C. F. Hurlebusch's *Compositioni musicali* intro-duced him to pieces no more than jejune, but they may have suggested to him a fugue-subject and other details to develop in his own masterly E♭ Prelude and Fugue. Faint echoes of Bach's involvement in 1736 with J. G. Walther's publication *Allein Gott in der Höh' sei Ehr* might be heard in one of the chorale-settings (BWV 676). And acquaintance over the years with certain French organ music (Grigny, Du Mage) could have suggested to him the idea of making a Lutheran equivalent to their liturgically planned *livres d'orgue*.

Perhaps receiving the title of Saxon court composer in late 1736 prompted Bach to produce a monumental volume of organ music to match the monumental choral works associated with this appointment (the Kyrie and Gloria of the so-called B minor Mass). Or, perhaps the volume followed on the composer's Dresden recital in December 1736 much as the *Musical Offering* was to follow on his appearance at the Potsdam Court – that is, he produced a publication reflecting what had been played and further worked on after the recital. This particular December organ-recital was in the new Frauenkirche, a unique church of great fame in 'baroque Germany', and the organ was a new and spectacular instrument by Gottfried Silbermann, of whose smaller organ in the Sophienkirche Wilhelm Friedemann was *titulaire* at the time – a position for which no doubt he too needed a repertory of pieces. Very different from *Clavierübung III* though his own best-known music turned out to be, Friedemann might well have played such organ music for church services, much as he was later to perform some of his father's cantatas.

Part III has the biggest and most complicated plan of all the volumes of 'Keyboard Music', containing clear divisions in the integrated whole:

the Prelude in E♭

a series of large and small mass settings (six Kyrie and Christe chorales, three Gloria chorales)

a series of large and small catechism settings (twelve, two for each chorale)

four *Duetti*

the Fugue in E♭

Twenty-seven pieces in all – perhaps one of the volume's many allusions to the Trinity (3 × 3 × 3) and to Lutheran orthodoxy. The mass settings represent Luther's reformed liturgy as the catechism settings represent Luther's reformed doctrine. There are many levels and types of intricacy in *Clavierübung III* which need fuller discussion elsewhere, but for present purposes one should be aware that the collection is an unsurpassed compendium of both pious and musical allusion, in some respects surely forbidding for musicians now as then – note the unique reference to 'connoisseurs' on the title page.

At least four major agendas are being played out here. First, the overall plan is much like that of an idealized organ-recital, with a massive ritornello prelude and final fugue in three sections, framing a series of liturgical chorales. This is a recital-plan such as one eye-witness of the period describes Bach as following in Leipzig, though the publication itself could have established such plans. Then the texts, including Luther's catechism hymns, rehearse orthodox liturgy and doctrine not in theory but in practical settings for organ, i.e. as pieces usable in actual services by a proficient ('practised') organist. The smaller chorales, though not necessarily easier to play than the larger, could also have served as devotional music at home. Thirdly, the music itself ranges from quasi-Palestrinian counterpoint (*stile antico*) to quasi-galant chamber trios, from French and Italian idioms to traditional German-Lutheran counterpoint, and as such offered a range of stylistic models or lessons for any composer.

And finally, the impeccable invertible counterpoint of the four *Duetti* and various trios, the two big-scale canons, and at least three distinct fugue-types (fughetta, ricercar, and a *Well-tempered Clavier* type) provide models of contrapuntal working superior to any handbook by any theorist. *There*, perhaps, lies a problem with the volume: one senses a calculated theoretical, didactic or even doctrinaire component to it. This component might be to some extent countered by a would-be modernity in some of the settings, but this is a modernity which nevertheless lacks the more artless melody of such music as the cantata-arias published for organ some years later (the *Schübler Chorales*). That during the broad period of composition Bach's students included several later prolific writers or, may one say, pedants (Mizler, Agricola, Kirnberger) could be a further element in the picture.

Details in the engraved (etched) plates, described in Butler, *Clavier-Übung III*, suggest the contents of the volume to have gradually evolved. According to such reasoning, it started with the mass and larger catechism settings; to these were added the Prelude and Fugue in Eb, along with the smaller settings (later 1738); and finally, in the middle of 1739, the four *Duetti* were introduced, amongst other things to fill empty space and to make up the number of pieces to twenty-seven. An aim of the volume was to include elements of French, Italian and traditional German organ music, with the texts in German but drawing on Latin and Greek originals. In this connection the composer may even have had in mind some allusion to a much earlier book originating (like Kuhnau's) in Leipzig, copies of which he owned: this was the keyboard music or

*Tabulaturbuch* published in 1571/83 by the then organist of St Thomas's, Nicolaus Ammerbach, whose title page promised German, Latin, Italian and French pieces.

Much more modern works too are relevant to *Clavierübung III*, of course. Since one of the Leipzig engravers working on the volume had also worked on another big chorale-collection of the time, Kauffmann's *Harmonische Seelenlust* of 1733, it is likely that Bach was well acquainted with it and possibly set out to supersede it with frankly better music – that is to say, with more substantial settings, more wide-ranging styles, a harmonic sense ever beyond a Kauffmann, some modern notational details (slurs, dots, *p* and *f* signs) and some learned archaisms (modal key-signatures for some pieces). Kauffmann had given organ-stop registrations for his chorales, and why Bach did not can only be guessed – perhaps because he had in mind 'serious' contrapuntal creations very different from Kauffmann's colourful and approachable settings of well-known melodies.

We should not forget that in his new volume Bach must also have been responding to himself – to his earlier organ music and its various approaches to setting chorale-melodies for organ. Thus, rather than the rapt and immediate beauty of the small-scale chorales of the *Orgelbüchlein* (1713–15), we now have instances of that abstract idiom that so often attracts composers in their maturity. And rather than the easy melody of some other early chorales, or the terse drama of many a youthful chorale-harmonization, we now have an earnest, spacious, almost distant majesty of expression, sometimes rich and dense, sometimes deft and light, sometimes calculated and always free of whimsy. The result in many of the pieces is a certain remoteness, and I think one could not regard *Clavierübung III* as 'superior' to the *Orgelbüchlein* in the way the harpsichord partitas are clearly an advance on the English Suites.

One interesting possibility emerges from the similarity between the Hurlebusch pieces and those framing *Clavierübung III*: Hurlebusch's are in D major, and the question arises whether this was the original key – in intention or in fact – of the great Prelude and Fugue in E♭. These are, after all, *organo pleno* or Full Organ music of a kind seldom found in such a key as this before equal temperament. The Prelude's unlikely passage in E♭ minor would then be in D minor, and throughout both pieces, D major or minor fits the hands better. In *Clavierübung II* as well, the composer seems to have gone to the trouble of changing the Ouverture's original key, presumably for an important purpose, but again one not explained. In *Clavierübung III*, would such a transposition be for the three flats to serve as yet another allusion to the Trinity? Or because the next piece (the first Kyrie) also has three flats, begins on a b♭ and therefore follows on better than if the Prelude had ended in D major? But if that were the case, and since in an actual Lutheran service the Kyrie would not follow straight on the organ's opening voluntary, might this be further evidence that *Clavierübung III* was indeed an idealized recital-programme?

## 'Clavierübung IV'

Within twenty-four or perhaps thirty months of Part III, Bach had had the *Aria with 30 Variations* published, and none of his buyers could have been prepared for the total change of musical personality between the two books. The very difference between them was unusual for a pair of keyboard books of the time, perhaps unique.

Whatever the precise dating of the *Goldberg Variations* – composed over 1739 to 1740, engraved during 1741, on sale at the Leipzig Michaelmas Fair 1741? (see Butler, 'Neues zur Datierung') – one imagines a certain *family aspect* to it in so far as the same engraver-publisher Schmid in Nuremberg was shortly to publish Philipp Emanuel's *Prussian Sonatas*, which are harpsichord or piano pieces of unmistakable modernity. (These too are hardly free of Rameau's influence, I think, although he is nowhere acknowledged by Philipp Emanuel.) About that time too Anna Magdalena copied the *Goldberg* Aria into her keyboard album, either from the print or from another, now lost copy by the composer. Strange, if the whole thing was already or about to be available at the time – perhaps the variations were beyond her, and it was the Aria she liked? Wilhelm Friedemann's likely connection with the work in Dresden has already been mentioned. Despite such possibilities, however, the work's compositional history is uncertain and various hypotheses on its early stages can be made. Three may be briefly mentioned.

The first is that the variety, extreme contrast, elements of caprice and sheer virtuosity of the *Goldberg* do make one think of Domenico Scarlatti, whose first book of harpsichord pieces had recently been published in London: the *Essercizi* of 1738. *Essercizi* is an equivalent of *Übungen*, and it is a curious coincidence that the volume contains thirty highly characterized sonatas, the last one contrapuntally ingenious. Little is yet documented on what London publications might have been known in Saxony in 1740, and the name Scarlatti appears only fitfully in the usual Bach literature. But still, it cannot be out of the question that the *Goldberg* was in part a response to that not very clearly organized book of Scarlatti, whose fabulous musicianship and playing technique are nevertheless clear enough from it. The opening and closing phases of the *Goldberg*'s structure are not very clearly organized either, if we assume the variations are numbered in the order composed, which nobody knows for certain.

A second idea is that since the canon at the ninth (No. 27) is the only true round in two parts, and comes only after all the other intervals in the octave are represented (see the list of movements below), it and movements around it have been added at some point. The 'original plan' might have been for twenty-four movements, formed around the other eight canons going up from the unison to the octave.[6] But in order to pursue this idea, other conjectures become necessary – such as that the French Overture halfway through was another late addition – for which there seems no firmer evidence than for other, and conflicting, observations one might make on the individual movements. More than one writer has thought that there are very good reasons for having nine canons (see below, p. 99), and no evidence has emerged to show that the work was or was not realized according to a scheme fixed in every detail before the composer began.

A third hypothesis is that one particular manuscript copy of Variation 5 is conveying an early form of it, apparently independent of the print, in which the notation is less detailed (the crotchets plain, without implied articulation) and some of the figuration seems to be in a form not yet finalized.[7] Seeing that more trouble is often taken with notation when a work is to be engraved and published – i.e. to make it more precise, as in the case of the Ouverture engraved and published in *Clavierübung II* – the hypothesis is just plausible. But there is no evidence whatever for dating this version, whose title is *Prelude*.

Whichever of these ideas might be usefully explored in further researches, the *Goldberg* as a whole is certainly to be seen as contributing to the repertory of keyboard music in a new way, by bringing into the public domain the idea of the unrepeatable or 'one-off variation cycle', complex variations of an unusual kind, clearly models in some sense and yet hardly imitable. One could not make such points about other variations then in print, by Handel, Couperin and Rameau, to name only the best. Though the polished work of gifted composers, their variations could conceivably have been matched by other sets of a similar kind, and Handel alone included nine examples in the seventeen suites of his first two books. (There are none in *Clavierübung I* and *II*.)

Also, the *Goldberg*'s incomparably elegant Aria has little in common with the conventional 4/4 *aria* of German variations as seen in the works of Pachelbel (*Hexachordum Apollinis*, 1699), Handel again (e.g. D minor, HWV 428) or even early Bach (the *Aria variata all [a] man[iera] italiana* in A minor). This last, Bach's only other set of harpsichord variations, seems far less a preparation for the *Goldberg* than do his other, bigger-scaled and unrepeatable compositions based on harmonic variation: the violin Chaconne, the organ Passacaglia and the chorale-cantata *Christ lag in Todesbanden*. The *Goldberg Variations* for harpsichord have more in common with the *Canonic Variations* for organ than with the early *Aria variata*.

But there are various other versions of the 'one-off variation cycle' from Bach's later years, and in each of them he was leaving far behind the realms of the readily imitable. The *Goldberg Variations*, the 'Fourteen Canons' (based on a common-property bass), the *Musical Offering* (fugues, canons and a whole trio-sonata based on Frederick the Great's theme), the *Canonic Variations* (canons around the melody of one of Martin Luther's chorales), and the *Art of Fugue* (fugues and canons worked from an original theme): essentially, all of these were dead ends, wonderfully instructive but hardly progenitive. To add to the fund of keyboard variations popular at the time, a highly reasoned plan like the *Goldberg*'s – with its symmetries, contrapuntal ingenuities, systematic array of genres and taxing technical demands – is surely to be seen as a deliberate attempt on the composer's part to 'raise the standards' then current.

In considering the four *Clavierübung* volumes as a group, there emerges a (so to speak) worrying question. In the middle of each volume, and nowhere else but here, is a piece in the French style – the *stile francese* as the editors of the posthumous *Art of Fugue* called it – complete with the characteristic rhythms and rhetorical gestures of a French overture:

| | |
|---|---|
| the 4th of 6 partitas in Part I | p. 33 out of 73 pages |
| the 2nd of 2 pieces in Part II | p. 14 out of 29 |
| the 14th of 27 organ pieces in Part III | p. 39 out of 77 |
| the 16th of 30 variations in 'Part IV' | p. 16 out of 32 |

(In the case of Part III, the frenchified movement cannot be a prelude-and-fugue as in Parts I, II and IV but has to be a chorale-setting.) The symmetry is there to be seen on paper and is probably more theoretical than practical: it need not mean that if one timed a performance of all the music, those pieces would hit the halfway point. But note that if this organization around a kind of musical pivot is not accidental – and it is hard to see quite how it could be – several things would follow.

First, the composer must have had a reason for it, and one can only assume that he was familiar with the rhetoricians' notion of the 'Inner Exordium': the idea that as one gives an extended speech (sermon, plea, address), it is effective to start again in the middle. Secondly, since Part I of *Clavierübung* – a combination of separate publications – has the least symmetrical pagination, perhaps Bach had not intended the patterning quite so literally at first, and/or then resolved to 'improve' on this with the later volumes.[8] Thirdly, since various engravers worked on the volumes, it looks as if the composer oversaw the production from this point of view, perhaps in each case (certainly Parts II, III and IV) leaving firm directions for the volume's eventual pagination.[9] And lastly, since the four French pieces have keys that make a particular pattern –

D major, B minor, E minor and G major

(i) D major is the relative of B minor, E minor of G major

(ii) D is the dominant of G, B of E

– either this is a coincidence or the *Goldberg Variations* are in G major not because of the associations of its bass but because more than a decade earlier a suite in D major had been published. But how can that be? Is it really possible that Bach took this and not some other standard bass because it was traditionally associated with G major, the key he needed for this pattern in *Clavierübung*?

## The 'Fourteen Canons', BWV 1087

In one extant copy of 'Part IV' there are a few markings in the hand of the composer (the, or a, so-called *Handexemplar*), which perhaps he was preparing for a later and improved edition. At the end of it, on the inside of the copy's outer covering page, the composer added fourteen brief perpetual canons in unrealized form, numbered 1–14 by him and entitled:

> Verschiedene Canones über die ersteren acht Fundamental-Noten vorheriger Arie. von J. S. Bach

> Diverse canons on the first eight fundamental notes of the preceding Aria, by J. S. Bach

*Fourteen* immediately suggests some kind of allusion to BACH (= 2 + 1 + 3 + 8 = 14), especially as there are actually fifteen pieces (No. 10 is double); similarly, an '*etc*' written at the end, which contrasts with *Fine* at the end of the *Goldberg* on the previous page, might mean that he could make more of them if he wished. But such points could also work against supposing an allusion to BACH. Besides, if number 14 is significant here, so then is number 10 for the rather similar-looking canons printed in the *Musical Offering*. Ten for the Commandments (*decem canones*) – if not, why not? If so, why?

Of the 'Fourteen Canons' twelve are in the modern 2/4 (popular for examples in theory books); one of them (No. 10) has more than one solution, none entirely without infelicity; and yet another (No. 13) has a simple countersubject almost certainly taken from Fux's well-known treatise *Gradus ad Parnassum*.[10] The handwriting is probably of 1747 or 1748 and is roughly contemporary with other canonic work of the composer, in the *Canonic Variations* for organ, the *Musical Offering* for chamber group and the *Art of Fugue* for keyboard. Whether as a set they were originally composed or compiled earlier – before or after the *Goldberg* – is not known, however, or whether they were intended for publication in a revised edition of the variations. But from a musical point of view, one could see the *Goldberg Variations* as 'extending' their short, eight-note theme rather as Purcell had pulled it out into a five-bar phrase or as Bach's organ Passacaglia had doubled the length of André Raison's original *passacaille* bass (see p. 38). With the *Goldberg*, of course, the 'extension' is on a more massive scale.

Although two of the fourteen canons survive in other copies, this is the only known grouping of them as a set, here a fair copy presumably made from an earlier draft. As with the *Musical Offering*'s canons, there is no extant realization of them by the composer. The very similarity of the wording 'diverse variations' and 'diverse canons' in the titles of the *Goldberg* and the 'Fourteen Canons' makes the latter look like a complement, in miniature, to the massive movements of the former, and the first four of them are as short as a diatonic canon can be. The little theme (eight simple crotchets) somewhat resembles the first line of the chorale-melody used for the variations, 'Vom Himmel hoch' (see Example 1), while its canonic techniques complement those of the *Musical Offering* – but again on a smaller scale.

Example 1

(a) Canonic bass of 'Fourteen Canons'

(b) Chorale-melody, 'Vom Himmel hoch', first line

The eight notes sound like a bass line and produce a diatonic progression so simple that one might think only a composer with certain preoccupations would take the trouble to write canons on it.[11] This Bach does with the apparent intention of giving a two-level survey of canonic types that are based on short repeated phrases of four bars and so serving as epitomes or *exempla in parvo*. The first musical level surveyed is that of canonic species, i.e. the settings progress from simple canons of eight notes against themselves to a six-part triple canon and a four-part canon involving augmentation and diminution – which one is left to find for oneself, like the 'Seek and ye shall find' canons of the *Musical Offering*.

The second musical level surveyed is figural species, i.e. the notes and lines range from minims to semiquavers, with conjunct or disjunct motion, plain or syncopated, diatonic or chromatic, with canonic intervals from unison to an octave-and-a-fourth. This sounds complicated, but the epitome-like nature of the bass-lines ensures so straightforward a sequence of tonic, dominant and subdominant chords that it is not too difficult to create lines that will move logically and combine convincingly. To write a canon above a given bass-line may sound supererogatory – the bass is an extra factor for the composer to take into account as he composes – but in fact this framework, if of such a basic type, is a help.

Clearly, some of these items of musical vocabulary also appear in the *Goldberg Variations*, but on a bigger scale. Particularly by the time the last of the 'Fourteen Canons' is reached, the counterpoint has worked towards the kind of musical sound that appears nowhere else but in canons – and is even there only *just* plausible.

# 2

## Overall shape

### The theme-type

The title, 'An Aria with diverse Variations', already produces a puzzle: if the thirty movements are variations on this aria or theme, why is it never heard again or even hinted at in paraphrase or some decorated form until it is repeated, *sans différence*, at the end? (Repeated but not written out: the player is told *Aria da capo è fine.*)

Of course, it is the harmonies underlying the Aria that serve as the basis for the variations, thirty distinct essays exploring the language and genres of music as its composer understood them. But when, during the century or so between Frescobaldi's and Handel's published sets, the theme of some variations had been called 'aria' or 'air' by composers, both its melody and harmony had been glimpsed from time to time. This was also the case with Bach's various other variation-works: not only in the early *Aria variata* and chorale partitas – where part of the point was to hear the hymn-tune, to be reminded of it, how ever subliminally – but so it is too in the mature *Musical Offering* and the *Canonic Variations*, where the themes continue to be 'glimpsed'.

Perhaps some players or listeners fancy that in the course of the thirty movements they do hear the original melody of the Aria now and then, but I for one do not and can only assume that one is not meant to: we have here variations or varied treatments not of a melody but of a series of chords, which are explored in a series of discrete genres and according to a uniquely ingenious plan. The Aria *itself* is one of the 'discrete genres', and some remarks on its distinctive character follow in Chapter 3. At this point, the focus is more on its bass-line and the harmonies produced by it.

Three especially important details are immediately clear from the bass-line as it is extracted and illustrated in Example 2, a line from time to time slightly displaced (chiefly in some of the canons) or replaced by another note in its harmony (as already in No. 1, second half). The three details are:

The 'theme' is curiously melodious, producing a line logical and singable; these characteristics bear on the sustained *melos*, the implicit melody, of the work as a whole. This is no 'mere' bass-line like the old or new passymeasure (passamezzo).

It appears to begin on the downbeat, in both Aria and all the variations. But note that the 'Fourteen Canons' do not (illustrated in Example 1 above); nor does the chorale-melody 'Vom Himmel hoch' with which it shares a family likeness.

Example 2 gives only the extracted bass: neither the Aria nor any variation has the bass-line so simply set out as here, and it is always 'coloured' more or less; it never appears plainly either as *ostinato* (as in the Passacaglia for organ) or as *cantus firmus* (as in the *Canonic Variations*), though some movements begin as if they might be of this sort; and some harmonies appear prominently in different inversions (hence some doubled notes in Example 2).

Example 2 Fundamental bass of the *Goldberg Variations*, showing alternatives in second half

Taken by itself, the bass-line would seem to most listeners to begin on an upbeat, so perhaps there is something of a 'metrical tension'

throughout the work. But it begins with a descending figure that then ascends to a cadence, which is an archetypal idea and one found in a variety of guises during Bach's lifetime, including of course the 'Fourteen Canons'.

In general terms, such a bass has a vast pedigree stretching back to various ground-basses circulating widely in the sixteenth century. All of these are explicitly diatonic – a simple framework of tonics and dominants, with perfect cadences – so much so as to suggest either that they helped establish the key-system of western music, or that the natural logic of the key-system made them inevitably popular and useful. For some versions of this generic theme taking a form similar to the opening phrase of the *Goldberg*'s, see Example 3. It is important to recognize that in its formation the theme is 'dialoguing with past music': the opening four notes have their own history as a recurrent bass in the seventeenth century; extending them to eight was common, as both Examples 1 and 3 suggest; doubling that to sixteen (to the halfway dominant), and then matching that by a mirror section (i.e. another sixteen, returning to the tonic) is itself a clear sign that squares and multiples of two lie behind the whole edifice. It is as if the *Goldberg* theme had begun as four notes, then became eight, then sixteen, then thirty-two.

Example 3

(a) Johann Christoph Bach, *Sarabande. duodecies variat*:

(b) Handel, Chaconne from Suite in G major, HWV 442 (see also HWV 435)

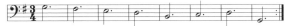

(c) Gottlieb Muffat, Ciacona from *Componimenti musicali* (*c.* 1739)

spiritoso

(d) Purcell, Ground in Gamut, Z 645

(e) Purcell, 'Let each gallant heart', Z 390 (transposed here from C major)

Note that in Example 3 (a), J. C. Bach (1642–1703) was already creating a sixteen-bar theme from the opening formula, with repeats perhaps misunderstood by the later copyist.[1] In the case of the *Goldberg* the eight-bar phraseology is driven by its own musical logic, with the first and last eight bars cadencing in the tonic, the second in the dominant, the third in the relative minor. The plan could hardly be simpler and is easily preserved even when for three variations it moves to the minor, ensuring a compulsive logic throughout thirty-two movements, a monument to the natural strength of diatonicism as it had evolved.

Note too in Example 2 that by quadrupling the eight notes of the archetypal theme into thirty-two, Bach was taking further what he had done in creating his Passacaglia in C minor: André Raison's original theme had had four bars, and was now doubled to eight.[2] Although in at least five *Goldberg* variations (Nos. 4, 12, 19, 22 and 30) the first eight notes are clear enough to look like a *cantus firmus*, the lengthening of a simple bass by a factor of four will remove any *ostinato* element it might have had, because the length will inevitably create full, independent and separate movements rather than a passacaglia or chaconne as such. The other eight-bar versions in Example 3 look like actual chaconnes, and are so treated by Handel and Muffat – note Muffat's direction *spiritoso*, which puts one in mind of Lully's chaconnes.

The first four descending notes could, and in the seventeenth century did, produce a variety of *ostinato* works, both in the major (the *ciacona* of Corelli's final trio-sonata, Op. 4 No. 12) and in the minor (Biber's *Passacaglia* for solo violin). By *c.* 1650 or so, these notes had become a standard way of producing long movements for Italian guitarists and French harpsichordists, partly or wholly in the minor and often chromaticized at some point. It would seem to be out of the question that Bach knew nothing of these various traditions and that his theme is entirely free of any allusion to them. The Corelli, also in G major, was almost certainly known to him, and since Muffat's *Componimenti* of *c.* 1739 was soon familiar to Handel (and rifled by him), so too it might have been to Bach, its fine engraving style perhaps encouraging him to be more than usually generous with ornaments and certain articulation signs, in the theme and occasionally elsewhere.

In Bach's 32-bar structure the traditional dance-style and idiosyncrasies of chaconnes are now quite lost, and none of the variations resembles in any respect a chaconne of the kind underlying Purcell's and Muffat's variations on the eight-bar bass (Examples 3 (c) and (d)). I imagine this was deliberate, and Bach cannot have been the only composer to feel that such a common-property bass required him to make an original gesture with it. In this respect the Purcell ostinato song (Example 3 (e)) is particularly striking, being a kind of reverse of the Bach approach, for it actually reduces the number of bars (from eight to seven), telescoping the second half to produce a charming and original version typical of its composer.

## The plan and its threes

As the outline below suggests, the variations are markedly different one from the other and, perhaps apart from the last five, not as continuous and their order not so inevitable as might be commonly supposed. Giving variations a marked character, so that they are not merely less or more flashy but different in tempo and style, was already attempted in Bach's early set of harpsichord variations, the *Aria variata*, which sources suggest was subtitled by him *alla maniera italiana*. What is Italian about these variations has always been rather a puzzle, but I think it could have been that they had different tempi and tempo-signs, unfamiliar in Germany but learnt by Bach from Corelli's *La Folia*, the last of the solo violin sonatas Op. 5 (hence *maniera italiana*). The differences of tempo in the *Aria variata* are not very pronounced and are mostly, as with Corelli, a matter of different tempo-signs and an articulation to match. But now, just as the *Goldberg* takes an old theme and extends it further, so it takes this principle of 'difference' farther and produces a full genre-mix, moving from one strongly characterized and independent variation to another. There was really no precedent for this, common though it has since become.

Nor was there for the overall plan, which can be found to be more complex than perhaps the composer intended, for so often what Bach wittingly plans can also unwittingly create various levels of pattern. Thus one can speak of two shapes for the *Goldberg*, a perceptual and a conceptual.

Perceptually, the movements proceed by way of great contrast and change, reach several kinds of semi-climax en route (particularly the French Overture in the middle), sink in the pathos of the long G minor Variation No. 25, build a crescendo of excitement towards the end (certainly as usually played), achieve festivity in No. 29 and a choral *tutti* in No. 30, and then die away as the Aria returns and eventually closes the work. Public performance as generally understood since the *Goldberg*'s period will most often require some such approach to the work, in which there is a sense of impetus and a tension achieved through music's passage in time and unavoidable transience.

Conceptually, however, there is a more static pattern, and one neither easily perceptible nor strictly transient, since it is always there on paper to be grasped. The thirty variations are made up of ten groups of three, in which a dance or clear genre-piece (such as a fughetta) is followed by an arabesque-like movement (bright, usually requiring crossed hands on two manuals) and this by a canon (created at successively rising intervals). The thirty variations are built up from a series of these threes which do not, of themselves, either create or remove tension: some are harder to play than others, but the gentlest might be some of the most intricate from a contrapuntal point of view. The overall shape of Aria–Overture–Aria approaches something of an arch-form with the 'biggest' movement in the middle. In that case, there need be no crescendo into the finale, and two manuals for No. 29 (such as the rubric offers) would be more delicate than one.

Players could reflect either shape, though hardly both, and the arch-form might be closer to what such a composer, in the days before standard public recitals, was looking for as an ideal.

The plan-of-three is disguised by the fact that some canons do not sound particularly canonic (Variation No. 3), while other movements do that are not (No. 2). Nor, with one exception (No. 27), are the canons simple rounds between two voices; rather, they resemble trio-sonata movements in which a bass accompanies the canon, therefore to some extent covering it and leaving the overall pattern as something conceived rather than perceived. The sequence is as follows:

| | | | | |
|---|---|---|---|---|
| 'Aria' | 3/4 | 1 man. | 3 voices | melodic, like a sarabande |
| Var. 1 | 3/4 | 1 man. | 2 voices | hand-crossing (a polonaise?) |
| Var. 2 | 2/4 | 1 man. | 3 voices | imitative, as a trio-sonata |
| Var. 3 | 12/8 | 1 man. | 3 voices | canon at the unison |
| Var. 4 | 3/8 | 1 man. | 4 voices | imitative, as a passepied |
| Var. 5 | 3/4 | 1 or 2 man. | 2 voices | hand-crossing, duet |
| Var. 6 | 3/8 | 1 man. | 3 voices | canon at the second |
| Var. 7 | 6/8 | 1 or 2 man. | 2 voices | dotted gigue ('al tempo di giga') |
| Var. 8 | 3/4 | 2 man. | 2 voices | hand-crossing, duet |
| Var. 9 | ¢ | 1 man. | 3 voices | canon at the third |
| Var. 10 | ¢ | 1 man. | 4 voices | 'fughetta' |
| Var. 11 | 12/16 | 2 man. | 2 voices | hand-crossing, duet |
| Var. 12 | 3/4 | 1 man. | 3 voices | canon inversus at the fourth |
| Var. 13 | 3/4 | 2 man. | 3 voices | melodic, like a *sarabande doublée* |
| Var. 14 | 3/4 | 2 man | 2 voices | hand-crossing, duet |
| Var. 15 | 2/4 | 1 man. | 3 voices | canon inversus at the fifth, minor |
| Var. 16 | ¢ | 1 man. | 2–4 voices | 'ouverture', followed by |
| | 3/8 | 1 man. | 2–3 voices | stretto fugue |
| Var. 17 | 3/4 | 2 man. | 2 voices | hand-crossing, duet |
| Var. 18 | ¢ | 1 man. | 3 voices | canon at the sixth, as a trio-sonata |
| Var. 19 | 3/8 | 1 man. | 3 voices | minuet? |
| Var. 20 | 3/4 | 2 man. | 2 voices | hand-crossing, duet |
| Var. 21 | ¢ | 1 man. | 3 voices | canon at the seventh, minor |
| Var. 22 | ¢ | 1 man. | 4 voices | 'allabreve', as a gavotte? |
| Var. 23 | 3/4 | 2 man. | 2–4 voices | hand-crossing, duet |
| Var. 24 | 9/8 | 1 man. | 3 voices | canon at the octave |

| Var. 25 | 3/4 | 2 man. | 3 voices | 'adagio' arioso, minor |
| Var. 26 | 18/16 | 2 man. | 3 voices | hand-crossing, sarabande filigree? |
| Var. 27 | 6/8 | 2 man. | 2 voices | canon at the ninth, a round |
| Var. 28 | 3/4 | 2 man. | 2–4 voices | hand-crossing, trills |
| Var. 29 | 3/4 | 1 or 2 man. | 2–3 voices | hand-alternating, as a *batterie* |
| Var. 30 | ¢ | 1 man. | 4 voices | 'quodlibet' |
| 'Aria' | | | | |

NB:  the groups are not marked as such in the score
words in the engraving (or the composer's copy of it) here in
quotation marks

That the first two variations reverse the usual order (a hand-crossing duet and then a genre-imitation) might suggest that the plan only gradually took its present form; but the final sequence is also irregular, resulting therefore in a symmetrically irregular framework. Perhaps the composer consciously broke the pattern to avoid too neatly calculated a scheme, or to make sure that the work begins and ends energetically, irrespective of any scheme.

A glance at the time-signatures alone suggests how maximum change is rung between movements. For example, the nine canons use eight different time-signatures, and the two that share ¢-time surely do so with a different tempo (No. 21 has a slower crotchet than No. 9). The word 'imitative' hardly implies the range of contrapuntal thinking involved, for what is imitated varies from a whole melodic phrase for No. 2 to a short persistent motif in No. 4. In each of the groups of three, the word 'hand-crossing' represents an unusual *étude* generally in 3/4 time, a virtuoso piece not at all like the Two-part Inventions or any other obvious genre. Certain not very pronounced similarities may be found between these movements and other virtuoso music of the period from Rameau to Philipp Emanuel Bach (1720s–1740s), and to this extent these of all movements suggest the composer to be deliberately working in up-to-date idioms – or trying to, as far as his personal taste would permit.

That *Clavierübung IV* has thirty variations $(3 \times 3 \times 3 + 3)$ while *Clavierübung III* had twenty-seven movements $(3 \times 3 \times 3)$ need not imply a significant connection between the two. But it is no surprise to find that the *Goldberg*'s thirty are more systematically planned than either the twenty-one or the sixty-two variations in Handel's two Chaconnes in G major, which use the same first eight notes of the bass-line, and in the same key. Nevertheless, there are certain parallels between the *Goldberg* and these sets, made probably some thirty years earlier. Thus the sixty-two variations, HWV 442 (oldest copy *c.* 1718), are headed by a theme or harmonized melody called 'Chaconne', and the last variation of all is a simple two-voice canon. By 1733, the work had been published in four printed editions, two of them in Amsterdam. In the other set (HWV 435, also called 'Chaconne'), which had appeared three times by 1733 and is somehow related to HWV 442 (sharing five of its variations), eight are in G minor. One of them has a decorative melody and is marked 'adagio'; the next (No. 10) includes a 'dragging motif', not rare in minor variations and found again in *Goldberg* No. 15. And in No. 16 Handel uses a descending Chromatic Fourth as in *Goldberg* No. 21 – a motif already used by Louis Couperin's *Passacaille* in G minor (*c.* 1650), based on the same opening four notes.

Some copies of Handel's vocal works were made by Bach in the 1730s and 1740s, perhaps giving a mere glimpse of the works which he knew and which led to his admiration of Handel, as reported in a later remark by Philipp Emanuel. But presumably the *Sarabande with twelve variations* by J. C. Bach (see Example 3) had long been known to his younger relative, even serving to suggest how a longer theme might be made of this bass, and prompting him to develop variations of a more careful, original and intricate kind. While actual resemblances with any of these works need not mean that Bach was consciously influenced, they certainly illustrate the kinds of tradition to which even the *Goldberg* is not indifferent. A variation like No. 21, at least as it begins, could well be a conscious essay in creating new music with an old motif.

## The plan and its twos

Some reference has already been made to numbers involving multiples and powers of two, and just as one soon becomes aware of the

patterning-by-threes in the *Goldberg*, so one can soon find a whole catalogue of binaries equally governing it. Thus, there are

2 halves to the whole work (one beginning, one ending with the Aria)

each movement is in 2 exact halves, each half played twice

2-bar phrase-structure

2 keys (major, minor)

also, 2 manuals

4 bars for sub-phrases of melody and harmony (to imperfect cadences)

8 bars for phrases of melody and harmony (to perfect cadences)

16 bars in each half of the theme

16 movements in each half of the work

32 pieces, 32 pages

a bass-theme of 32 bars (or notes)

all movements notated in 32 or 16 bars (both in No. 16)

I imagine that other allusions to powers of two could be found, including the German terminology for note-values: halves, quarters, eighths,
sixteenths and thirty-seconds. (Tovey calls the four-bar phrases 'qua-
trains', a useful term.) One little detail in the print confirms the idea that
No. 16 begins the second of two halves: in the engraving, this variation
alone has its first bar inset, after the clearly written title 'Ouverture' – a
discreet hint that could have been made much more obtrusively had the
composer wanted to drive home the symmetries. As with the fact that,
after all, thirty-one movements and not thirty-two are actually written
out, one might assume that the composer had little interest in making
everything obvious. Musically speaking, however, the opening of No. 16
could not be more startling or more obviously a change of direction after
the unusual fade-away of No. 15.

Note that to have a binary movement in two exact halves (16, 16 bars)
was not at all common at the time and unlikely to arise by chance. Perhaps
Bach remembered the two Sarabandes from Rameau's *Livre* of 1706
(8, 8 bars), and the *Goldberg* Aria was alluding to a fixed sarabande-
type; or, since he had already created exact halves in the Allemande

and Courante I of the English Suite No. 1 (which themselves recall the opening Allemande of Louis Marchand's *Livre* of 1702), he recognized the attraction of symmetry. Otherwise, binary movements almost always have the second 'half' longer, hence (amongst other things) the natural evolution of Sonata Form during the eighteenth century, foreseen in the Sarabande of Partita No. 4.

Also by no means as typical of music of the high baroque as one might suppose is the conspicuously clear two-, four- and eight-bar phraseology in every movement. It is very striking throughout the *Goldberg*, and yet the composer is not dominated by it, nor is the continuity of each movement ever threatened.

The connection between diatonic tonality (music in major/minor keys with perfect cadences) and the two/four-bar phrase (music with a cadence at regular intervals) is a matter for consideration elsewhere, as too is the question whether either is innate and 'basic'. But at least one can recognize the *Goldberg* as confirming once and for all the power of both. Of course, there would be a danger to any composer in over-separating phrases, especially two-bar ones, and scattered throughout are joins and half-joins, particularly the overlapping phrases in the canons. But once aware of this detail – one hears it as the work begins, a wistful melody already shaped like a question and answer – the listener soon relishes the skill with which the composer marks off two-bar phrases while still leaving the music continuous enough that one barely notices them.

To a greater or lesser extent, the effect of the canons is to thwart the otherwise familiar four-bar phraseology with their overlapping phrase-ends, and it seems unlikely that they appear as regularly as they do in the *Goldberg* without this being intended. In such movements as the canons at the fifth and seventh (Nos. 15 and 21), the overlapping is one of the features contributing to their elusive character, counteracting the four-square phraseology of the previous variation.

## Some further general points

To return to the idea that the work is no mere abstract pattern, patent and inartistically doctrinaire: one can see that several of its essential characteristics work to prevent it becoming so. The opening and closing irregularity of the dance–arabesque–canon sequence; the sheer difference in musical genre between the movements, irrespective of their part in the sequence (e.g. whether or not they are canons); the exploring of both twos and threes, both to the ear and the eye; the irregular placing of the minor variations and of the slow movements; the variety in the arabesques (not always two voices) and canons (not always three); the absence of other symmetries that would have been easy to organize (e.g. if the canons at the perfect fourth and fifth are *inversus*, why not the canon at the perfect octave?) – such properties leave an element of caprice not always obvious in the works of Bach.

The most obvious and simple element of symmetry in the work – the Aria framework – does allow for all kinds of grouping for the movements. Thus, quite strict fugal movements are found at regular moments (Nos. 10, 16 and 22), and the sequence of canons rising by step from the unison through to the ninth is clear on paper if not always to the ear. At the same time, many movements begin with a kind of atavistic allusion back to the genre *chaconne* for their first eight bars, and only gradually move away into a quasi-independence – 'quasi' because they still follow the harmonies if not the actual bass-line. The opening eight bars alone serve as a kind of memorial to old G major chaconnes.

Also strictly observed – though this is not a matter of symmetry – was the need to find thirty-one genre-pieces (i.e. including the Aria) which have or could have no upbeat. No allemande or courante was possible in this scheme, therefore, nor were conventional passepieds, bourrées and gigues. Sarabandes, minuets, polonaises and (had they been wanted) marches were possible, however, as were gavotte-like or gigue-like movements as long as one omitted written anacruses. The arabesques, being lively movements in triple time with only a certain amount of motivic imitation, might in theory resemble *perpetuum mobile* courantes or correntes such as that of the Partita in G major, but in fact they have few if any obvious antecedents.

The overall result of all this is that not only is the *Goldberg* quite distinct from standard decorative variations of the day, but it makes no attempt to order or shape a sequence of movements so as to resemble a suite – surprisingly, perhaps, for after No. 16 the next variations could have been dances as in a true *ouverture*, including the B minor Ouverture of *Clavierübung II*. I am not even sure that the existing movements most like suite-dances – the sarabande, passepied, minuet, *giga*, gavotte – are immediately recognizable as such in the stream of variations. Knowingly or not, the listener is affected by the bass-theme to hear the variations as variations. The one movement to have upbeats – the last, No. 30 – does so because the tunes opening each half are not the composer's.

In the *Musical Offering*, the 'Fourteen Canons', the *Canonic Variations* and the *Art of Fugue*, the canons are grouped together: not merely on paper but also (at least, for the second and third of these) as a performable group. This appears not to be so in the *Goldberg*, where the numbering is unambiguous, and one is given no encouragement to pick out the canons and make a separate sequence of them. Because of the canons, one could regard the whole work as built up in two ways: three kinds of variation are set ten times; or there are ten groups of three variations, in each of which the hardest contrapuntal task is achieved in the third piece, and the hardest to play is the second.

If one views canon as the hardest to compose, then the fugal movements that sometimes form the first of a group of three – Nos. 10, 16 and 22 – are to be taken as less demanding from a composer's viewpoint. Other groups, as in Nos. 1, 2 and 3, show an increase in the contrapuntal strictness (1 free motifs, 2 imitation, 3 canon) while in the group Nos. 25, 26 and 27 the music becomes progressively lighter towards the canon. In fact, generally the various groups of three take very different shapes, as if they are meant to remain conceptual and not be perceived as groups of three. At the same time, since the last four virtuoso movements for two manuals (Nos. 23, 26, 28, 29) have more voices than the earlier (Nos. 5, 8, 11, 14, 17, 20), there is a perceptual buildup in the virtuoso group. While this might follow the simpler keyboard variations of the day in becoming more difficult and exciting as they proceed, in general the shape of the *Goldberg* contradicts anything so straightforward. One of the hardest variations to play well is actually the first.

The Quodlibet is clearly conceived as a grand finale to the set of canons, especially after the thin-textured one at the ninth (No. 27). The canons have been varied in such details as which voice comes in first (the top or the middle); at what interval of time a voice is canonically answered (half a bar, one bar or two bars); and whether the voice-answering is reversed (first the lower answers the upper after a gap, then the upper answers the lower after a gap, thus eating up the bars). This last was presumably an ingenious way of dealing with knotty harmonic problems. In any case, treating the principle of canon so variously and using so many different time-signatures are surely signs that the composer was aiming at a *survey*. The eight canons that pass from the unison to the octave display a further symmetry: unison, then second, then third, then *inversus* fourth are followed by *inversus* fifth, then sixth, then seventh, then octave. Perhaps there are other allusions, as with the canon at the ninth for movement No. 27 (three squared and three cubed). In several ways, this last canon is exceptional (no bass), redundant (there is already a canon at the second), and in a sense isolated (there is no canon at the tenth). Perhaps this encourages one to suppose (with Breig, 'Goldberg-Variationen') that the work was originally conceived with twenty-four variations only, but then one has to guess which variations were added and conjecture why. It does seem to be the nature of the *Goldberg* to inspire a range of hypotheses.

On a more down-to-earth level, some points may be made about the nature of the keys of G major and G minor. Whether or not the key was chosen for 'strategic' purposes (see p. 32), G major seems to produce a certain family likeness in Bach's keyboard works in the decade or so before 1740: see Example 4 for a group of similarities in the handling of a two-part texture in 3/4 time. In such examples I would not claim more than a family likeness, and in no way impugn the astonishing invention of the composer, but many such instances might be heard by the player. Or perhaps 'felt', since it is a question here rather of how the fingers are placed and how they feel as they negotiate the figuration in a particular key. Seldom are the motifs actually identical, and more striking is how different are similar ideas at similar moments, considering their family likeness. Even for something so simple as a closing bar, one example might have a running scale (the G major Prelude, *Well-tempered Clavier* Book 2) while another doubles it in contrary motion (*Goldberg* No. 1).

Example 4

(a) Variation No. 1, bb. 25–7 and Praeambulum, Partita in G major,
   BWV 829 (bb. 69–71)

(b) Variation No. 5, bb. 13–14 and Prelude in G major for organ,
   BWV 541 (bb. 63–5)

At least twice, G minor as it appears in the *Goldberg* reflects habits
associated with the old *tonus secundus* (the church mode becoming the
key G minor), particularly in chaconnes. For just as Louis Couperin's
*Passacaille* in G minor moves to G major in the course of the variations
and, like Italian instrumental music of the period, eventually chromati-
cizes the bass by way of further variation, so Bach too employs all three

basses, major, minor and chromatic. The chromaticization is clearest in No. 21, shown here in Example 5. There is no direct link with Louis Couperin but there certainly is with the general tradition in which he was working, a tradition clear again in Handel's variations in G major, HWV 435, as mentioned above. Although at the beginning of *Goldberg* No. 5 the descending and ascending four notes are not yet chromaticized, the unique *Affekt* of the *arioso* 'adagio' Variation No. 25 is founded on one Chromatic Fourth after another, paraphrased descending (bass, bb. 1–4), staggered ascending (tenor and bass, bb. 13–16), both ascending and descending (bb. 10–12), and so on.

Example 5    Variation No. 21, opening

## Remarks on the notation

In addition to its unique plan and achievement, the *Goldberg* can be recognized as being something of a pioneer in its notational details. As remarked already, it seems that in preparing a work for publication, J. S. Bach gave it more fine points of notation than he might have done in a copy circulating in manuscript. This alone may explain (as suggested above) why the Ouverture in B minor of *Clavierübung II* has 'sharper' rhythms than its manuscript version in C minor, or how it comes about that an organ chorale with a uniquely high number of articulation signs appears in *Clavierübung III* (the larger 'Vater unser' setting, BWV 682). It is possible that if the final chord of a work is short and all the rests carefully written in (as with the B minor Praeludium for organ, BWV 544, or the C major Fugue, BWV 547), it was intended for publication; and conversely, the long final chords common in manuscript copies (most of *Well-tempered Clavier* Book 1) need not be taken literally.

In several details of notation, the *Goldberg* stands out among its period's publications. Firstly, the two directions *a 1 Clav* ('for one manual') and *a 1 overo 2 Clav* ('for one or two manuals') are, I think, unique, and though so worded as to be obvious antitheses to *a 2 Clav* (long used by organists for lines of a chorale), they are really rather strange. No-one needed to say a piece was 'for one manual', and would do so only for special reasons, such as (a) wishing to give every variation its own rubric or (b) using *1 Clav* to mean 'any or all sets of strings' and *2 Clav* 'two separate 8′ sets'. There is no precedent for either, however, and although German harpsichordists were not much used to two manuals, as organists they would have known that *a 2 Clav* meant 'use two manuals if they are available'. Curiously, the Aria has no rubric but must be a one-manual piece although the right hand has a solo melody: the accompaniment goes on to the upper staff where necessary and the cadential chords are divided between the hands, neither of which is so for the obvious solo movements Nos. 13 and 25.

Secondly, although two manuals are required, there are no *forte* and *piano* signs such as are found in *Clavierübung II* and regarded as *de rigueur* for two-manual music by the time of e.g. Philipp Emanuel's organ sonatas of 1755. Nor are there any echoes or directives to change manual for expressive purposes, as was the case already in Rameau's *Livre* of 1728/9 and perhaps in *Clavierübung III* (E♭ Prelude).[3] Although the two melismatic variations Nos. 13 and 25 certainly use the two manuals expressively, i.e. for a melody above accompaniment, there is no indication for *forte* and *piano*, as there had been for a similar layout in the slow movement of the Italian Concerto. In short, the notation of two manuals in the *Goldberg* is *sui generis*, not quite following convention in any respect.

Thirdly, though only in certain variations, there are more slurs and dots than one finds in such contemporary engravings as Scarlatti's *Essercizi*. Slurs are presumably for purposes of articulation, closely related in the longer examples to violin bowing (as in No. 13); and dots can be added to indicate equal or non-lilting semiquavers (as in No. 16). These are shown in Example 6. In the nature of harpsichord touch, one would also expect the dots to indicate *détaché* rather than *staccato*, but something approaching the latter must be the case in the brilliant Variation No. 14, and even a *quasi-sforzando* for an isolated dot in No. 28, bar 31. (The last seems also the case in the *Duetto* in G major, recently published in *Clavierübung III*.) The 'dragging motif' of the minor Variation No. 15 is the opposite of this, its slurred pairs of notes very like those in some older and rather conventional chorale-preludes for organ, and presumably always to be played with some exaggeration, whether rising or falling, in order to evoke some sad *Affekt*.

Example 6

(a) Variation No. 13, bb. 11–13

(b) Variation No. 16, bb. 8–9

Finally, important principles of articulation are implied when notes are written short and (unlike Scarlatti's) followed by a rest, especially when there are longer notes without rests elsewhere in the vicinity. This is the case in No. 5, shown in Example 7. Note that an apparently earlier manuscript version has simple crotchets throughout, without this notated articulation (see Tomita, 'Early Drafts'). Since presumably the leaps involved here would always have had to be played *détaché*, it is the implied slur over the barline – i.e. where there is no leap – that is interesting and full of implication. Note too that for this kind of detail, here and in the other two-manual variations throughout the *Goldberg*, an especially brilliant tempo is not required, and it could well be that today's modes of concert-playing have distorted the original nature of such music, appealing overtly (as in most current recordings of the Brandenburg Concertos) to the tastes of the consumer-audience.

Example 7    Variation No. 5, opening

Of course, a major question especially for the performer is how far the explicit slurs, dots and note-values in a few of the *Goldberg* movements are to be understood as implicit in movements that do not have them. The little slurs of Nos. 5 and 14 are particularly important in this respect, since comparable motifs or figuration are found elsewhere, and one would dearly have liked the very different counterpoints of such variations as Nos. 16 and 17 to carry some hint of the composer's articulation. It could be that when they do occur, the slurs and dots are to be very marked, exaggerated even. But otherwise, and in general, one can surely assume that J. S. Bach tended towards a singing style of playing, given the singing style of his tunefully modulated lines, a phraseology constantly based on two and four bars, and an interest in what he had previously called *cantabile* playing.[4] This would not result in a characterless uniformity if the contrapuntal lines were articulated or phrased independently, but it might suggest that much harpsichord-playing of the twentieth century has been ill-judged and inappropriate.

# 3

## The movements

### Aria

That the Aria is not the theme but itself a variation – or, rather, a melodious and rich setting of harmonies accompanying a certain model bass-line – has been noted already, and given the *Goldberg*'s aim to create self-contained movements of a very distinctive character each time, a question is, What kind of piece is the Aria?

In some respects this is obviously a generic *sarabande tendre*, with leisurely pulse, slow harmonic rhythm, harmonies made from the full triads, various emphases on the second beat of the bar, a singing melody, no upbeat. Like Christoph Bach's simpler Sarabande (see Example 3, p. 37), the Aria also has a single chord at the end of each half (the traditional French sarabande has a feminine cadence with two chords, strong–weak), and again like it and older sarabandes generally, it gives a series of broken chords to the left hand.[1] (But older sarabandes of Christoph Bach's kind were much more lively and sprightly than those of Bach and Handel.) Starting with a quite high right-hand solo and moving towards more continuous and melodious semiquavers in the last half-dozen bars are characteristics that can be found in several of the sarabandes of the French Suites. There as here, one might have the impression that the piece before one is a *sarabande doublée*, i.e. a fluent variation of a chordal, perhaps richly chordal, original. One could imagine an 'original' sarabande something like that in Example 8, though so straightforward are the harmonies that in trying to reconstruct something of this kind, it seems impossible to avoid banality. The more one tries to extract such an 'original', the clearer it becomes that the Aria must always have taken the present form, including a left-hand part more imaginatively written than that of many an earlier sarabande. Further on in the *Goldberg* (Variation No. 26), there is a much richer sarabande-like setting, though it remains characteristically hidden and understated.

Example 8  Aria, bb. 1–8, reduced to a simple sarabande

For examples of how conventional semiquavers dominate or take over a written-out *doublée*, Bach's earlier sarabandes in the A minor and D minor English Suites offer case-studies. In the case of *Clavierübung I*, the six sarabandes make a point of stretching the dance's defining characteristics beyond any others by any other composer, and naturally they have room for at least one sarabande that looks like a *doublée* for which an 'original' could be hypothetically reconstituted (Partita in C minor), and another that hovers around a high right-hand melody (Partita in D major).

The Aria melody, particularly as it begins, is an exquisite example for the claim that all beautiful melody has a tinge of sadness or (as I would prefer to say) transports us to a world of imagination always inclined by its transience towards melancholy. In ornaments and style of *cantabile*, the movement is not totally removed from the sarabande of the G major French Suite, and some telling little comparisons will strike the player of both – for example, the two-bar phraseology of the Aria becomes all the clearer when set against the four-bar phraseology of this sarabande, which likewise melts into semiquavers. Also, in the earlier piece there is a relatively unthinking quality about, say, its cadential bars or its modulation to the relative in the second half – in comparison, that is, with the Aria, which a close look reveals to be at every point curiously lacking in formulas and ready answers. The slurs look as if they are there to prevent a perky way of playing the shorter notes, implying a long line in the right hand (as in the French Suite in C minor), which the unusual notation of bb. 27–30 confirms as being *sostenuto*. The long appoggiaturas, either as written out in b. 1 (a″–b″) or as a grace-note in b. 2 (e′–d′), conform with the style of a neo-galant sarabande such as had already appeared in the D major Partita.

The striking melody and attention-demanding gesture that open the series of G major variations-on-a-bass in Handel (HWV 435) and in Muffat (*Componimenti*) are absent from the *Goldberg*'s sweetly lyrical Aria. Did its obvious gentleness inspire Forkel's insomnia anecdote? Note that its opening high *cantabile* suits the early fortepiano, like the beginning of the Ricercar à 3 of the *Musical Offering*.

## Variation 1

The idea that this might be a polonaise is a guess, based only on certain details: a dance in steady triple time, the gestures, the feel of 'swing' in both the quaver and the semiquaver figuration, the dactyls, the downbeat anapaests in the first bar of each half (cf. the Polonaise from the E major French Suite). But there is admittedly little in common here with the half-dozen polonaises in the second *Anna Magdalena Book*, where the characteristics of a rougher dance – the emphatic beat, the feminine cadence, the cross beats, blunter textures – are often more evident. There too, however, there is a polonaise in F major which had a variation in the form of BWV Anh. II 117b, and it does not seem out of the question to see Variation No. 1 as a more suave version of this idea: a two-voice *polonaise doublée* on a fundamental bass.

The genre is nevertheless elusive. The angular lines and their invertibility suggest more a binary sonata movement for violin and continuo than a two-part invention: something related to a *Duetto* from *Clavierübung III*, perhaps, or distantly related to the kind of Allegro found in Handel's keyboard works (e.g. F major Suite, 1720), which is derived from binary *perpetuum mobile* toccatas then becoming popular in Italy and sometimes called 'Sonata' by Handel. The alternating four-bar phraseology is consistent in the first half (1–4 inverted in 5–8, 9–12 in 13–16) but happily breaks down in the second, where the last six bars form one intensive phrase on the analogy of the close of the Aria. The hand-crossing of bb. 21–2 recalls Rameau, but the originality and detail of the piece are undeniable – as unusual as the figuration is exciting and idiomatic for the player. The one-bar phrases that characterize much of it (as in Example 9) are an interesting example of the composer's double agenda: to give players the pleasure of some inner, held-in rhythm (a kind of controlled jazziness) and at the same time to appeal to their connoisseurship (in the first half this sequence falls, in the second it rises).

Example 9    Variation No. 1, bb. 9–11

## Variation 2

In No. 2, what looks very much like two violins over a steady cello-bass becomes so close to creating a true canon that one is bound to wonder if Variation 2 inspired Variation 3, the first canon. A trial run for the canons? The stretto rising between the two upper voices in the last quarter of the variation, however, is more that of an idiomatic violin duo than of canonic counterpoint. The close imitation and crossing remind one of such music as Corelli's *ciacona* in the Trio in G major, Op. 4.

The semiquaver motif that has emerged fully by b. 8 is then heard in virtually every bar, including the bass running into the final cadence. Meanwhile, this bass part has created its own quaver motif (b. 1) and sticks to it as much as is compatible with genuine music, even though the second quaver is a dissonant auxiliary note (see particularly bb. 9, 14, 21). Such exhaustive treatment of various by no means simple contrapuntal motifs recalls the composer's techniques in *Clavierübung III*, as a bass that is more than a mere bass anticipates the Sonata of the *Musical Offering*. One can find a similar motivic ingenuity in several movements of the three publications.

## Variation 3

The first canon is bound to create closely crossing parts between the two right-hand voices, since it runs at the unison. (The ear has been prepared for this by the last few bars of No. 2.) It also means that the harmonic bass has to be contracted or repeated to reach the dominant by b. 8, and sometimes, this left-hand part seems to be sustained only by the composer's sense of melody. Perhaps this canon was the first to be written, and the nature of the third voice had not yet evolved – as the canonic interval widens in the course of the variations, the left hand has to participate more in the canon.

Curiously, the two voices hardly need a bass and are self-contained – or would be if the fourth of b. 14 were re-written – and while the bass certainly helps create a piece of harpsichord dance-music (especially in b. 1) it goes on rumbling about to no great purpose. It only gradually breaks out from the magnetic Gs of bb. 3–5, and only in the second half produces a bass-line of Bachian conviction. The canonic answer is differently harmonized this time, and there is less repetition of the harmonic bass, the underlying *Goldberg* harmonies being more varied in the second half.

There is another important motif: the six semiquavers, heard twice in the first bar and infiltrating all three voices by the end of the movement. Yet there is also something of a plethora of motifs in No. 3, a certain note-spinning which may give the effect of a continuous rolling useful in a variation, but doing so without the imaginative single-mindedness of the next variation.

## Variation 4

At this point the variations have still not settled down into their clear groups of three. Rather, No. 4 gives the impression of being another motivic *tour de force* like the previous three variations but more so, i.e. a dance constructed this time on only one note-pattern. It is not a difficult pattern to work and is accordingly found in almost every bar, either *rectus* or *inversus* – increasingly *inversus* – in any of the voices and sometimes in several at once. See Example 10 for typical samples. This motif is surely as naturally *détaché* as that in No. 3 is slurred or *legato* – a difference that does not appear by chance, doubtless.

Example 10    Variation No. 4, bb. 1–3 and 21–3

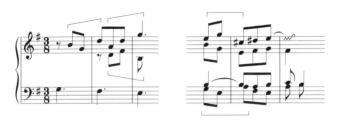

The composer's interest in creating music by working little motifs, such as can be discerned in every movement of *Clavierübung III*, has already been mentioned, and it does lead to a question of whether something of this kind was the or an original idea for the *Goldberg*. Was it planned at first as a demonstration matching *Clavierübung III*, showing how to create idiomatic and useful harpsichord music (to match the earlier organ chorales) by means of tight, motivic counterpoint? And as part of this, was the idea to include some accompanied canons at appropriate moments in both volumes – for reasons of symmetry in the *Goldberg* and for reasons of textual allusion in *Clavierübung III*? Neither book is simply a collection of popular pieces for the usual customer.

The motif illustrated in the last example is not the only one in this fine dance. Another conspicuous one declares its resemblance to passepieds in Bach works: Example 11 shows one, and there are others in *Clavierübung II* (the Ouverture in B minor). That *Goldberg* No. 4 is no true passepied, however, is a consequence of the composer's self-given restriction in the work as a whole. For although it has the hemiolas characteristic of passepieds,[2] it should ideally have an upbeat, preferably on the tonic. Either way, since the 3/8 of No. 4 may be much the same in tempo as the 3/8 in No. 3 (or livelier?), the harmonic rhythm has speeded up dramatically: every strong beat moves to the next note of the bass theme.

Example 11

(a) Variation No. 4, bb. 19–20

(b) English Suite in E minor, BWV 810.6, bb. 9–11

## Variation 5

With No. 5 we seem to have reached the first of the regular two-voice, hand-crossing 'arabesques'. But only *seem*, because the rubric actually gives one a choice of one or two manuals – quite possibly an indication not only that the groups of three movements were not regular at first but that the composer was not so pedantic as to go back and tidy up possible discrepancies from an earlier stage of composition. The *Handexemplar* (a copy used by the composer) slurs pairs of quavers in b. 19, as in b. 18, but these make sense only on two manuals.

Hands cross more often here than in No. 1, though not as consistently so as in some other variations. For a note on the articulation implied by the notation, see above, p. 52. Here again one finds wonderfully idiomatic figuration for hands on the keyboard, and here again there are reminiscences of other works in G major – the Prelude in the *Well-tempered Clavier* Book 2, for instance (see bb. 6–7, 11–12, 27, 29–30 of the variation). The movement is a fit partner to the Praeambulum of the Partita in G major, higher praise than which is inconceivable. In theory, the handling of the two parts faintly recalls textures perfected by Rameau or Scarlatti, or hesitantly approached by the Telemanns of the day; but one would be hard put to find anything like it anywhere else.

Nevertheless, despite the originality of this conception, a technical detail should not be missed: here, in the bass notes, is a particularly clear exposition of the *Goldberg* theme. Since its main notes appear on the main beats, one can easily pick it out, just as one can the hymn-melody underlying many a paraphrased line in organ chorales, at least amongst Bach's earlier works. (In its paraphrases of chorales, *Clavierübung III* is much more intricate.) The idea of keeping the original notes of the chorale-melody on the beat while in between appear any number of decorative notes is familiar in Buxtehude and Pachelbel, to name but two, and is here adopted not for a hymn-tune but for a 32-bar bass.

## Variation 6

The dashing canon at the second is rather of a piece with the canon at the unison (No. 3), but in No. 6 the bass is better integrated, joins in the canonic voices' semiquaver motifs, develops its own, and has a well-timed change to quavers just before the end. This movement is, from a composer's viewpoint, a clever, convincing and very polished achievement; and from a listener's, a rich *perpetuum mobile* of cascading semiquavers. Note that the canonic theme begins with, and largely keeps up, the passepied motif identified in the last example (Example 11), and, not for the only time in the *Goldberg*, tension is created by some contrary motion (bb. 17–22).

A canon at the second can be organized, as here, to produce a string of suspensions on the beat, and not the least remarkable element contributing to the fluency of No. 6 is that every main beat, except at the cadences, is a suspension needing resolution. (There had been very few suspensions in the canon at the unison.) The *Goldberg*'s bass-theme as such rather disappears, for the composer takes its harmonies and presents them in whatever inversion fits the suspensions of the canonic voices. There are also in this variation some very deft chromatic touches decorating the basic harmonies, producing what Tovey aptly calls 'an exquisite passage', an 'example of the power of expression which strict canons sometimes can give' (Tovey, 'Goldberg', p. 45). See Example 12. These chromatics are the first to appear in the work, and keep up, as one can see, the many suspensions.

Example 12    Variation No. 6, bb. 9–13

## Variation 7

Many a player must have been surprised some years ago when the composer's copy of the *Goldberg* turned up and it was discovered that he had marked this movement 'al tempo di giga'. For it had always seemed to some (though not to Tovey) that this was a siciliano, gentler and more lyrical than a gigue of the dotted French type. Perhaps contemporaries had thought so too, and the added rubric was meant to remove ambiguity. The rubric saying 'giga' rather than 'gigue' must be because there was no common term *au temps de*, and *tempo di* had already been used in *Clavierübung I*, apparently to imply that the piece was a 'character piece in the time of' rather than 'the dance called'. Since one might think *à la manière de* (or an Italian equivalent) a more appropriate phrase, perhaps tempo was the main clue to genre, for Bach as it might have been for Couperin. Did the exact halves of the *Goldberg*'s binary movements disqualify them from being called, simply, gigue or passepied?

No. 7 is a dotted gigue of the same kind as found in the French Suite in C minor, where too the left-hand part is closely related to the right. Both it and the C minor gigue pick up the right hand's patterns and develop them, more than one would expect in an Italianate pastorale or siciliano. There is less imitation between the two voices in the dotted gigue of *Clavierübung II* (the Ouverture in B minor), though there one does also find the little melodic demisemiquaver runs of *Goldberg* No. 7, if now without slurs.

The option to play it on two manuals anticipates the two manuals for the canon at the ninth (No. 27): relatively simple pieces in which the two voices share motifs and melodic character. Clearly, the left hand of No. 7 is more of a distinct bass-line, but its derivation from a shared motif or two (e.g. bb. 8–9) conforms to the composer's general preoccupation at this time. Every music student would benefit from studying the left-hand part of this variation and taking in the total command it has of melodic contour, motivic counterpoint and pressing harmonic movement.

## Variation 8

Amongst all the fireworks of No. 8, one could easily miss the fact that it is taking the *Goldberg*'s two-bar phraseology a step farther by dividing it into one-bar phrases. This is consistently kept up, even when the left hand counteracts the flow by running down to the end of the first half with a much longer phrase – which is later reflected in the right hand's run down to the final cadence.

Though to us vaguely reminiscent of certain Scarlatti *essercizi* and ultimately related to other duos of the period such as the *Duetti* from *Clavierübung III*, the two-hand conception of this movement is startlingly original. It has been planned to produce an overlap of lines on three occasions, very challenging to the player and just comfortable in the stretch; and its main motif (the first four semiquavers) can be extended and inverted simultaneously against itself as well as admit a new countersubject late in each half. When the lines are not crossing, the left hand is unmistakably a bass, with its quaver pattern spelling out the *Goldberg*'s bass-theme on the main beats (see especially the first eight bars). In this, and in its angular motif, the left hand recalls a much earlier kind of duo – the old chorale bicinia, such as 'Allein Gott', BWV 711, where the paraphrase-technique (Example 13) is already sophisticated. *Goldberg* No. 8, like bicinia, Inventions and *Duetti*, is yet another contribution to the sheer range of two-part music.

Example 13   Chorale, 'Allein Gott in der Höh' sei Ehr', BWV 711, showing the notes of the melody

## Variation 9

A subject beginning on the mediant and answered in canon at the third below could lead to repetitious harmony and thus changes in the *Goldberg*'s
harmonic scheme. For the first time, it becomes difficult in this variation
to trace the original bass notes, even though both the general direction
and the cadences – tonic, dominant, relative, tonic – are clear enough.
Particularly in the second half, modulating accidentals modify the answers (e.g. bb. 9–11), creating with the Neapolitan sixth in b. 11 a meta-
morphosis of the canonic subject, much like the kinds of chromatic change
made to the subject in some mature fugues – the D major Fugue, *Well-
tempered Clavier* Book 2 or the Fugue in C major for organ, BWV 547.

The cleverness lies not so much in the harmonic ingenuity as in
producing a variation of distinct character and forward movement
irrespective of the difficult canon. Since thirds are consonant, there
are likely to be fewer discords on the beat than in a canon at the second; but since, too, a different canonic line could have been devised,
we can assume the consonances of Variation No. 9 to be quite deliberate. Unlike the canon at the unison, it seems to me to have neither the
'remoteness' of canonic harmony nor its typical cruxes; and unlike the
canon at the tenth in the *Art of Fugue* (BWV 1080.16), it does not wander
around aimlessly, thanks to its driving bass-line and a logical binary form.
The skill with which the canonic subject (upper voice) rounds off each
half with a pretty cadence while allowing for the answer below (bb. 7–8,
15–16), is intensely musical: a model for the student and a pleasure for
the player.

The gentle binary movement that is No. 9 even begins rather like a
Corellian Andante, with a cello bass inclined (as often in trio-sonatas)
towards more activity as it approaches the cadences. This is common in
the *Goldberg* and has the effect of marking off each half and so emphasizing
the binary divisions, especially when repeated.

## Variation 10

In his theory book of 1777, a former Bach pupil, Kirnberger, mentioned
the canons of the *Goldberg* and remarked that one of the variations was
'even a regular four-part fugue' (Dok III, p. 231), evidently something

to wonder at. In fact, however, the challenge here was not as severe as for some of the canons. The first four bars of the *Goldberg* bass can be paraphrased to make a fugue-subject; this can be answered in the dominant so long as it is a tonal, not real, answer (i.e. is not truly in the dominant); this in turn is answered back in the tonic (to match the bass-theme's harmony), and then in the supertonic (*ditto*) to close in the right key at the halfway point; and only for the final entry in each half will four parts be reached. If the fugal entries come at every four bars, the regularity itself will mirror the *Goldberg* bass, and a similar plan can be adopted for the second half, where one will hardly notice the oddity of two answers at the second (starting at B and answered at C♯ and then D). The last entry will even have the effect of a mini-recapitulation and thus of finality (compare tenor bb. 29–32 with bb. 5–8).

That the fugue-subject paraphrases the bass-theme in a catchy *alla breve* style is an extra bonus of the piece, recalling (anticipating?) one or two of the *Well-tempered Clavier* Book 2, and a great pleasure to play. The fughetta's four-bar or four-square phraseology clearly expresses one of the *Goldberg*'s ruling ideas and in no way attempts to modify the binary form, as a fugue might. Observing the strict framework was clearly part of the fun. A characteristic touch is that the running bass in the second half springs from the original countersubject (compare b. 17 with b. 5) and – another characteristic of mature Bach – could have been more narrowly derivative than it actually is (e.g. the quavers of b. 4 could surely have reappeared during bb. 21–4).

## Variation 11

The complex trills and 12/16 time-signature may appear at first sight to suggest a livelier or more brilliant style for this duet than is likely to emerge from a careful playing of it. Players are now often encouraged by the notation to play it 'presto possibile', but a comparison with the Prelude in B♭ major, *Well-tempered Clavier* Book 2, causes one to doubt that this is right: a steady, lyrical manner is not out of place in Variation No. 11.

In figuration, No. 11 is not unlike the Prelude in B♭ major, and in probably being more or less contemporary, the two can be seen as exposing a pair of motifs similar to but different from each other's:

descending on the beat in the first, off the beat in the second, both when the semiquavers are scalar (conjunct) and when they are leaping (disjunct). If one does see these two movements as a pair, the fact that No. 11 is shorter, for two voices only, almost entirely void of chromatics and geared to create maximum hand-crossing would be not accidental but the result of deliberation. So would be the distinct pairing of motifs, conjunct (b. 1) and disjunct (b. 5), corresponding to the elementary but fundamental distinction made by seventeenth-century theorists between the the motif moving by step (*passus*) and moving by leap (*saltus*). See Example 14 for this clear distinction as it is found in these two similar works of Bach's maturity, both of which also explore them in stretto. While Variations Nos. 5 and 8 had concentrated on one semiquaver motif for their 'arabesques', there is now in No. 11 a marked exploration of two.

Example 14

(a) Variation No. 11, b. 1 (conjunct) and b. 5 (disjunct)

(b) Prelude in B♭ major, *Well-tempered Clavier* Book 2, b. 1 (conjunct, off-beat) and b. 9 (disjunct)

Whether, therefore, No. 11 is less lyrical and more brilliant than the Prelude in B♭ is an open question. Not only does the use of two manuals suggests a certain delicacy, but virtuosity in 1740 may well have been less extreme or theatrical than a century later, when, as now, a passive audience expected to be entertained with polished brilliance. I imagine that most harpsichordists of the time were only just practised enough in hand-crossing to find the last half-dozen bars easily manageable.

## Variation 12

Like another canon at the fourth, in the *Musical Offering* (BWV 1079.3c), this is answered *inversus*: the subject is put upside down for the answer. (Or, to put it another way, the *dux* or leader is answered *inversus* by the *comes* or subordinate.)

None of the canonic phrases begins on a main beat, something that doubtless makes it less difficult for the counterpoint to follow the *Goldberg* bass – which itself is unusually clear throughout the variation and especially at the beginning. It disappears somewhat towards the end of the first half, where the bass-line 'justifies' the canonic harmony perhaps rather more complicatedly than it need (e.g. why would not three crotchet As do in b. 15?). But equally 'unnecessary' is the chromatic touch in the *dux* of bb. 24 and 26, and one may well suspect that the composer took particular pleasure in the *comites inversi* of the following bars. Perhaps it was these that gave Tovey a sense of 'droll capriciousness' in this variation ('Goldberg', p. 54).

Harpsichord touch is particularly suited to the left hand's full-length repeated crotchets at the beginning of this variation, which, combined with the dactyl rhythms and the prominent Gs and Ds in the opening bars, do rather suggest another polonaise. The very sophisticated canonic technique and motivic lines could be seen as countering the more rustic nature of polonaises found in the *Anna Magdalena Book* (see above, p. 56). Played with something of a swing, and a deliberateness in its articulation, this variation, like No. 6, again achieves what is so difficult: a stylish dance that is its own *raison d'être* irrespective of its canon.

## Variation 13

Below the beautiful lines of this particularly ornate *sarabande doublée* is a left hand – both chords and bass-line – which makes the clearest variation yet on the original Aria, or at least on *its* left hand (compare the opening eight bars of each). But this movement is not merely imitating the Aria's texture; it rises, falls and hovers with a melody as immediate as the Aria's, only now with a rhetoric that is almost verbal.

Precedents for such a decorative movement are less obvious than might be thought at first. The sarabande from the Partita in D major has a somewhat similar right-hand part, but it is not so exclusively for a second manual and its harmony is thinner. Closer in the second respect is e.g. the sarabande from the French Suite in G major, and it looks as if Bach often saw decorative melodies as appropriate for sarabandes. The slow movement of the Italian Concerto also springs to mind, though this variation, No. 13, is in the major and its expressiveness is not quite so heart-on-sleeve. As so often with Bach, certain parallels in the cantatas can be found for this movement, particularly arias whose *obbligato* solo instrument – violin, woodwind, even organ (BWV 169.3) – plays filigree patterns in the treble. These patterns often have motifs similar to those found in No. 13: turns (b. 1 etc.), syncopated *figurae* (b. 9 etc.), violinistic patterns (b. 13 etc.) and slurs (bb. 19, 32 etc.). With such characteristics and associations, No. 13 will be something like a solo for violin or oboe d'amore in a meditative cantata aria, with the range of feelings aroused or invoked by that kind of music.

## Variation 14

If No. 11, the previous variation with crossed hands, had already progressed to employing not one but two different patterns for the hands, how many more patterns are to be found in No. 14! After the meditation of No. 13, now sheer high spirits: the brilliance and virtuoso demands turn to an array of two-manual effects, patterns crossing, chasing and coming together – clearly, a very different use of two manuals from that of the previous variation. Again, however, this movement does not need to be played 'presto possibile'.

The four-bar phraseology is marked by changes of texture: bb. 1–4, jumping right hand; 5–8, crossed hands; 9–12, criss-cross; 13–16, imitation and concordance. This is followed exactly in the second half but *quasi inversus*, the hands the other way around. The temptation for players, to which I would encourage them to submit, is to play *legato* whatever is not *détaché* – which is not much.

The group of variations Nos. 13 to 16 stand out somewhat for their slurs and dots, suggesting a clearly marked performance style for each. So after the violinistic figuration of No. 13, No. 14 has snappy motifs that bring out a *détaché*, *staccato*, and even *sforzando*, which contrast with the slurred *cantabile* phrases in bb. 3 and 19. The sequence of Variations Nos. 13, 14,

15 and 16 gives new meaning to the idea of difference: there can never have been such marked contrast between four consecutive variations, not even in sets like the *folia* variations of Corelli or Couperin (1700, 1722). The nearest thing to a precedent could well be the Violin Chaconne.

## Variation 15

Again like a canon at the fifth in the *Musical Offering* (BWV 1079.3d), this is in contrary motion: the line is answered *inversus*. And again, as in Variation No. 12, none of the canonic phrases begins on a main beat.

So well is the bass-line now integrated into the canon that it imitates the canonic lines (e.g. the first beats of bb. 5, 6 and 7) and seems largely derived from the canon's motifs (e.g. bb. 17, 24). As was the case with the last canon, the bass of No. 15 repays a particular, close attention: it is immensely skilful and musical, masterfully disguising the fact that e.g. between bb. 8 and 11 the harmony barely moves, and creating a melodious sense of direction in lines that could easily have remained quite static. Note that when the second half moves to E♭ major, as is more natural in a G minor movement than the original E minor would be, the change is also modal: the beauty of E♭ *major* in this context cannot be missed.

The rubric 'andante' is not without difficulty. The slurred falling semi-quavers of the opening and recurrent theme – the so-called 'dragging motif' – can be likened to patterns familiar in organ chorales, not only recently in *Clavierübung III* ('Dies sind', BWV 678) but nearly forty years earlier in the *Orgelbüchlein*, where 'O Lamm Gottes', BWV 618, is marked adagio. Example 15 compares the motifs. But the chorale – which also has a canon at the fifth, in the chorale-melody – is in ₵-time. Perhaps 4/4 adagio is the equivalent of 2/4 andante, and both indicate a slow-but-moving crotchet beat. No. 15 has continuous semiquavers with some smaller groups (as does BWV 618) and it remains unclear whether andante is a warning against taking it too fast or too slow. Nor does the word seem to indicate a specific genre, quite in the way that later rubrics – *ouverture* (No. 16) and the *allabreve* (No. 22) – in the *Goldberg* do. Yet perhaps it does: this is a slow binary movement typical of the period's chamber music, something like the Andante from the *Musical Offering*, where the 'dragging motif' is less continuous.

Example 15

(a) Variation No. 15, opening

(b) Chorale, 'O Lamm Gottes, unschuldig', BWV 618, opening

↑ pedal (canon)

From a playing point of view, No. 15 is a valuable *étude*. While that word is usually reserved for the flashy two-manual 'arabesques' of the *Goldberg*, quite as useful for the studious player is the opportunity No. 15 gives for realizing counterpoint sensitively, marking each line with its own touch and articulation and working out versatile and melodically conceived fingering (e.g. left hand in b. 14).

From a formal point of view, there does seem something uncanny and inconclusive about the way this variation closes: a very open fifth, the last notes clearly the end of a canonic phrase, left floating like the last voice in a children's round. (The closing fifth is in fact a twenty-sixth, very unusual.) If in a modern concert an interval is taken here, the conceptual plan of the whole, in which No. 16 immediately restarts the continuous sequence as dramatically as possible, is disguised.

## Variation 16

Like both the Italian Concerto and the B minor Ouverture of *Clavierübung II*, No. 16 opens with a left-hand bang, the biggest chord of the *Goldberg* so far, a *tutti* like the *organo pleno* opening *Clavierübung III*, and thus in all respects as different from Variation No. 15 as it was possible to be. The B minor Ouverture was also as different as it could be from its preceding work, the Italian Concerto, but in another way: the textures were much the same but the key was as far away as possible. The *Goldberg*'s contrast is exactly the reverse of this.

Not the least witty detail in this perfect *ouverture à la JSB* is that the *Goldberg* bass, otherwise very clear in the dotted 'prelude', is suspended at one point by a long appoggiatura (bass b. 10, g–f♯), exactly as might have happened in a Parisian overture. Also, the bass is elided at the halfway point, so that the fugue begins over the last note of the prelude. With one exception (see next paragraph), all of the idealized French characteristics are here, the runs, jerky half-beats or quavers, rushed upbeats, even the thematic semiquavers of bb. 8–9, whose dots must indicate that they are both *égal* and *marqué* (see remarks above, p. 51). In addition to this, the *Affekt* is clearly different from that of the elegiac B minor Ouverture, being bright and largely free of the latter's weighty appoggiatura chords on the main beats, such as had also somewhat coloured the D major Ouverture that begins the second half of the six partitas of *Clavierübung I*.

An exception to the 'all-French' details as Bach had applied them in the D major and B minor Ouvertures of *Clavierübung I* and *II* is that the fugue is succinct, no longer than the prelude section, and does not have a chance to develop usual ritornello episodes. However, succinct fugues in French ouvertures had long been familiar to the composer – ever since he had copied out Dieupart's *Suittes de clavessin* (1701) over the years 1709–16. Here in the *Goldberg*, the fugue's beat is presumably the same as the prelude's (crotchet = dotted crotchet), so the bass-line's harmonies move at roughly the same speed. But only approximately, because the relative minor cadence in the middle and especially the sequential passage leading towards the final tonic both stretch and squeeze the harmonic progression, producing what looks like a free composition. In this respect, the fughetta of No. 16 is interestingly and consciously different from that of Variation No. 10, which strictly follows the four-square phraseology and admits of no 'freely inspired' composition such as we have here in the last ten bars or so.

The subject and its treatment are once again rather passepied-like, but a particularly French detail is starting the triple-time subject on a weak beat, a mannerism preserved in many *ouverture* fugues of Bach, Handel and others – as if the first violins run off into a dashing fugue, as indeed they often do. Example 16 shows two instances of many. The exposition is in three voices, the fleeting entry of a fourth (b. 23) signalling a change of direction, as the theme's modulation to E minor has to be preserved. More entries are possible than actually occur, and not for the only time in the *Goldberg*, the last section achieves a sense of finality through piling up or lining up the subsidiary motifs, here taken from b. 18. Why the last bar is notated in the metre of the dotted prelude, I do not know, but this was also the case in the ouvertures of both the D major and the B minor Partitas. The latter is so because it goes on to a 'postlude' section after the fugue that recalls the 'prelude' before it. Perhaps the *Goldberg* No. 16 is being faithful to its genre in – rather obscurely – implying that an *ouverture* returns after its fugue to its beginning. In any case, the full chords at the end of Variations Nos. 16 and 30 are the clearest finals in the *Goldberg*, reinforcing the middle and end of the work as a whole.

Example 16

(a) Variation No. 16, bb. 16–18

(b) Ouverture in F major, BWV 820.1, bb. 18–21

There is a further little detail offering insight into Bach's fidelity to his genre-models: note how the first time, the prelude ends with a full chord but the second time has only open octaves, which then shoot off into the dashing fugue. This difference is already to be found in the early Ouverture in F major, BWV 820 quoted in Example 16, and in Handel's equally early Suite in D minor, HWV 448.

## Variation 17

No. 17 is a useful reminder that one will often find precedents for particular motifs or thematic ideas of J. S. Bach in genres quite different
from the one in hand. Thus the way the hands run down together from
bb. 5, 13, 29, and therefore at other moments in the variation, recalls
similar moments in his much earlier arrangement of a Vivaldi concerto,
BWV 973. See Example 17. Since the Vivaldi is also in G major, it is
quite possible to find there other pre-echoes of *Goldberg* figuration – for
instance, for the scales of Variation 23. In general, it is likely that these
many concerto-transcriptions played a bigger part in forming Bach's
repertory of keyboard figuration than is now recognized, as is also the
case in the organ music.

Example 17    Concerto in G major, BWV 973.3, bb. 58–60 (from Vivaldi,
Concerto in G major, RV 299)

In addition, the two conspicuous motifs of No. 17 both appear in the
first sonatas in Scarlatti's *Essercizi* of 1738: its broken thirds up and down
are not unlike those in Scarlatti's Sonatas Kk 4 and 15 (particularly in the
left hand), and its falling broken sixths resemble similar patterns in the
Sonatas Kk 2 and 5. Similarly, the written-out pedal-point trills of a later
variation, No. 28, could have been prompted by Scarlatti's, in another
sonata (Kk 18). Of course, they did not have to be, but the point of

such comparisons is to suggest that a German composer could well have felt 'authorized' by such a splendid publication (appearing in a foreign capital) to publish similarly flashy music. On the other hand, if there is any likelihood that Bach knew the *Essercizi*, one is bound to wonder why he did not make use of some of its other patterns, such as the chopping arpeggios of Kk 24 or the repeated notes of Kk 26.

The continuity of semiquavers, which is rather a challenge to both hands, hides the regularity of the four- and two-bar structure. By now, the hand-crossing is fully developed and is able to serve as a contrapuntal element in itself – precisely because the lines appear to go their own way. The result is rather strange music, for while the broken thirds do have the bass theme's notes on or near the strong beats throughout the whole variation,[3] more so than one is immediately aware of, their line wanders up and down the keyboard and cuts free of the anchoring effect felt in many other variations.

## Variation 18

Despite their both being wonderfully idiomatic keyboard music in three voices, the canon at the sixth could hardly be more different from the canon at the fifth (No. 15). Because of the difference in mode and tempo, the *Affekt* has changed; and because of the tightness of its canonic stretto (the answer after half a bar), No. 18 is a more succinct and determined movement. Conventional 7-6 suspensions between the canonic voices (a natural circumstance with canons at the sixth) constantly drive its motion forward, with no lingering. And the dactyl rhythms and bourrée-like bass-line help to create a true *alla breve* movement, quite the opposite of the previous andante.

Why Variation No. 22 should be so similar in style to No. 18 is not clear, unless it was intended as a symmetrical 'reflection' of No. 10, being placed six movements after the *Ouverture* (No. 16) as the other is placed six before. Their style is not very far removed from the fifth species of counterpoint in J. J. Fux's *Gradus ad Parnassum* (1725), perhaps at that very moment being translated into German by Bach's former pupil, Lorenz Mizler, who published it in Leipzig shortly after the *Goldberg*.

Nos. 18 and 22 certainly strike the player as having more in common than either variation does with other *alla breve* movements of the period around 1740, such as the Fugues in E major and E♭ (*Well-tempered Clavier* Book 2) or any of the examples in *Clavierübung III*. Perhaps No. 18's least common characteristic is the reliance more or less entirely on the dactyl rhythm, expertly worked and mostly without dissolving into continuous quavers, as tends to happen with other dactylic *alla breve* movements, such as the same E♭ Fugue or the Ricercar à 6 in the *Musical Offering*. But unusually, the binary form here is emphasized by the two halves ending with the same eight bars.

The chromatic touches in bb. 14 and 30 modify the prevailing *Goldberg* bass, but this had in any case taken on a new character in the movement: the notes are there in each bar but not consistently in the bass, being scattered amongst all three lines, including the canon. However, the four-bar sectionality is clear enough, as of course are the various tonal centres, so the overall effect is still that of a variation on a theme.

## Variation 19

No. 19 is also succinct, with each bass note lasting one short bar. Opinions as to its 'true character' are often strongly held: whether it is a minuet (a kind of three-voice version of the minuet-type found in the Partita in B♭) or something much more boisterous is not obvious, but it certainly elicits from the player one or other kind of stylish approach. Whichever it is, No. 19 is surely a welcome respite before No. 20.

And whatever else it might be, No. 19 is certainly another motivic *tour de force* of great orginality. The inner semiquavers of b. 1 and their extension in b. 3 provide a note-pattern for every bar of the piece, sub-tly changed in profile and at no point pedantic or tedious. Given that the accompanying voices tend to be simple, the achievement is all the greater, reminding one of the charming *manière* and invertible counter-point of the Three-part Inventions. There is also an interesting relation-ship to the previous variation: both have many tied notes over the barlines, but the changes are rung between the possible suspensions, and one is hardly aware of the artistry involved. Example 18 shows the right-hand part at similar points.

## Example 18

(a) Variation No. 18, bb. 13–16
(b) Variation No. 19, bb. 13–16
(c) Fundamental bass

# Variation 20

As the virtuosity of the crossed-hands variations in the *Goldberg* gradually becomes unleashed, one is reminded again of Scarlatti, of Vivaldi
transcriptions (see remark concerning No. 17, p. 73 above), of the tradition for flashy improvisations shown in e.g. Handel's earlier free preludes,
and of the new keyboard tastes circulating in the 1730s. A painstaking
trawl through such sources would probably yield other examples of the
three invertible patterns combined in No. 20: alternating hands in crossed
arpeggios, a hand leaping over the other's triplets, bubbling lines testing
the player's hand-positioning. But the regular phrases (first eight-, then
four-bar phrases) and Bach's irrepressible interest in developing note-
patterns (compare b. 15 with bb. 30ff.) result in a movement one would
never mistake for any sonata or toccata by anyone else.

Two particular points concern the symmetry and the bass-theme. First,
the similarity between the two halves is marked at both the beginning and
end of each. This alone gives balance and unity even though the second
half has new virtuoso material and alters some of that from the first half
(compare bb. 9ff. with 21ff.). This alteration is partly in the interests
of some chromatic colouring, which has been rather absent from recent
variations. Secondly, the theme is still largely there on the first notes of
each bar, and thus still preserves some sense of the paraphrase technique
familiar from various kinds of chorale-setting.

# Variation 21

More than vaguely reminiscent of chorale-settings too is the next movement, the canon at the seventh, for the prevailing semiquaver patterns
in its canonic lines, and their habit of passing into the bass to create a
unified web of sound, look like a matured version of the kind of thing
Bach had been doing with chorales for forty years or more. The opening semiquaver motif is one found, in various forms and taking different
shapes (as it does in this variation too), throughout the composer's music.
Example 19 (a) gives an excerpt from an early set of variations in which
a theme (here in the treble, not the bass) is paraphrased with varied patterns of smaller notes, though the parts are even more uniformly derived
in the canon of *Goldberg* No. 21. It so happens that in this particular early
chorale chromatics are not prominent, but they might have been, because
the opening chromatic bass-line of Example 19 (b) was widely familiar
in all kinds of music (see remarks above, p. 50).

Example 19

(a) Chorale Variations, 'Sei gegrüsset, Jesu gütig', BWV 768, Variation
    No. 2, opening

(b) Variation No. 21, opening

Once again, the welcome calm of a more tender variation belies its
immensely deep musical thinking. The chromatics might be traditional

in principle, but their working is not: from single descending crotchets at the beginning to ascending quavers in imitation (bb. 3, 7), to syncopations (bb. 9–10), and then to inturning semiquavers (bb. 15–16) – this is a typical Bach progression. The beautiful effects resulting from imitation at the seventh in b. 9, or from 'justifying' the awkward canon in general during the second half, must have been a pleasure to the composer, even more than the effortless way he creates – and had long been used to creating – varying shapes for the semiquaver patterns (compare bb. 1, 5, 9, 13). One can respond easily to the beauty of this movement and barely notice that in fact the bass theme is not only there in every half bar but somehow still managing to be largely in the major:

G F♯ E♮ D B♮ C D G
G F♯ E♮ A F♯ G A D
D B♮ C **B♮** G A **B♮** **E♮**
C **B♮** A D B♮ C D G

Only the notes in **bold** are changed (flattened). Perhaps even the Neapolitan sixth in the last bar is significant, for then the last two notes of the canon (tenor g a♭, treble f♯′ g′) have the same interval, momentarily *per giusti intervalli*. One can never be sure to have grasped all of Bach's allusions.


## Variation 22

This *alla breve* movement sounds hardly less canonic than its predecessor (No. 18), but like Variation No. 4, it is four-voiced and densely imitative, parts of its subject heard in one or other voice in every bar, including the last of each half. As such, the movement is in principle not far from the motet conception of several major chorale-settings in *Clavierübung III*, where a *cantus firmus* is part of the texture. For a moment, in its opening bass notes, it looks as if this Variation No. 22 is going to have such a *cantus firmus*. Although it gives up the semibreves, only once is this bass deflected from the *Goldberg* theme, and that in the interests of the main motif and its suspension (b. 29), clearly suggesting that the composer kept the overall harmonic movement in mind while focusing on the logic of his motifs.

So in the course of three movements scattered through the work we have fugue, canon and motet based on material similar *sui generis*, though by no means identical. The last, for example, is the one to suggest most clearly the *Goldberg* theme in its bass. All of them are lively, engaging pieces, neat, succinct, catchy, not a bit church-like in tone.

## Variation 23

As for Beethoven in the *Diabelli Variations*, so for Bach in No. 23: extraordinary effects can be created with music's basic elements, particularly simple scales – lines tumbling over each other, answering or running against each other, both up and down, catch-as-catch-can figuration, split up or decorated, single notes or thirds or sixths, and any sequence or combination of these. While the four-bar phraseology remains intact, the rest is held together by being derived almost entirely from major scales. Off-hand, one would be hard put to think of further ways of making use of scale-fragments, given the language of 1740, and the result is spectacularly original, full of a reckless humour that affects the player. Can this really be a variation on the same theme that lies behind the adagio No. 25?

The opening tail-chasing is strongly reminiscent of Rameau's rondeau *La Joyeuse* in his 1724 book, where he wittily varies the interval and point of imitation while remaining light and faux-naif. There is no hand-crossing here, however, nor are two manuals called for.

While the two later Variations Nos. 25 and 28 somewhat explore chromatic motifs and lines, the only chromatic touch in the present variation (bb. 21–2) actually recalls an earlier, No. 12 (compare bb. 21–2 with No. 12, bb. 24–5). As with Nos. 17 and 20, this is a two-manual 'arabesque' sufficiently unlike other music of its period for one to be at all sure how virtuoso it actually is, i.e. how fast and brilliantly it is to be played. For instance, the alternating hands in b. 24 distribute the falling patterns much as they did in organ praeludia half a century earlier, but the latter are more sedate than harpsichordists think No. 23 is. However, since most passages are less demanding than they look, except for the final scales in contrary motion (prophetic of later music), perhaps in using two manuals for this alternation No. 23 does imply the 'presto possibile' approach.

# Variation 24

The canon at the octave in the *Art of Fugue* was called by the composer 'Canon in Hypodiapason', but *Goldberg* No. 24 is both *hypo* and *hyper*: first, a canonic line is answered at the octave below (bb. 1/3), then a second canonic line is answered at the octave above (bb. 9/11). Naturally, as by now one has come to expect, this order is reversed in the second half (first *hyper* then *hypo*). The 9/8 metre, vaguely pastoral in quality, produces a long line for a canon, and it is possible that since changing the order means fewer phrases to answer canonically – two long ones in each half – the composition becomes more manageable. The canon too becomes more immediately audible than some of the others. But it is also possible that Bach worked a longer theme in order to allow switching of octave answers.

Either way, No. 24 is wrought with amazing musicianship. Thus, while switching octaves meant he did not have to treat one of the treble phrases canonically (bb. 7–8), he nevertheless took pains to introduce it else-where, moreover doing so twice (bb. 15–16 and 31–2). That 'twice' also means that each half ends not only similarly but with material al-ready heard, thus giving the impression of a mini-recapitulation of the subject – which had also been worked on in the 'development section' (i.e. the first section of the second half). And the result of that is a very in-tegrated movement. To the listener, there is a single topic or *Affekt* here, as there was not in the previous variation: a sustained and delicate rocking motion familiar from other mature works of Bach written in a somewhat pastoral 9/8. There too might be found the lightly touched bass notes of this variation (in the E♭ Prelude, *Well-tempered Clavier* Book 2) and similar semiquaver patterns (C major Prelude for organ, BWV 547). Example 20 suggests, however, that these parallels never quite produce the same treatment of a particular theme or motif, even when as here both are mostly worked above a tonic pedal-point. One could begin to think that all J. S. Bach's composition was founded on the principle of variation.

Example 20

(a)  Variation No. 24, end

(b)  Prelude for organ in C major, BWV 547, end

pedal

It does seem fairly obvious that the last bars of this variation, involving reiterated tonics, the unmissable unwinding of a motif, and the unusual bottom Gs, sink towards a kind of inertia. In a performance, this means a fine preparation for what comes next.

## Variation 25

The 'adagio' mark added by the composer in his copy only confirms what must always have been obvious, that this is a slower and more intense movement than the *coloratura* variation No. 13 or any other moment in the *Goldberg*. The tempo is rather similar, I think, to that of

'O Mensch bewein' in the *Orgelbüchlein*, as is its grip of listeners, compelling them to find words or images for its pathos.

The *Goldberg* bass is now chromaticized but still within the 'rule' of one chord or note per bar. When, as before, the original cadence to E minor in the second half now becomes one to Eb, it is for the moment minor not major – a spectacular transformation. But then the picardy third allows an easy slip into the relative (C minor), and hence a return to the opening melody now on the 'south side' (subdominant). The result is a movement approaching classical Sonata Form in having two subjects (the second returning in the tonic, b. 28), with something approaching a modulatory development (first eight bars, second half) and something approaching a recapitulation (of Schubert's kind, starting in the subdominant).

The beauty and dark passion of this variation make it unquestionably the emotional high point of the work. Yet the technical means of achieving such rhetoric are almost simple and recognizably conventional, if now worked to new ends. The rising minor sixth at the beginning, for example, could be found in any cantata with a text of longing or languishing, but not I think the minor sixth of b. 2, which creates a false relation that will never fail to startle – and startles even more when it produces Bb minor in the second half. In fact, the right-hand melody throughout is as full of flat inflections as any aria of the day could be. Note that even in the approach to the D major cadence in the first half, there are still Ebs, and that throughout the variation there are little semitone drops in the melody – down from Bb, Eb, Ab (the astonishing note in b. 2), Db, Gb, Cb and even Fb (b. 23). Sometimes the lyricism becomes sharper, more acidic, with well-placed little chromaticisms; and sometimes it falls inexorably, down to the first cadence in b. 8 and especially over a six-fold sequence at the end. Where else is a motif heard six times to such effect? Where else do rising appoggiatura octaves take on such expressiveness, already in b. 5 but especially to the high D near the end? And where else is a grace-note made quite as dissonant as it is here at the end (evidently first time only), when on one manual it clashes with its resolution on another?

The harmony too has the extraordinary knack of being unconventionally conventional, the benefit of a lifetime creating exceptional music from common-property motifs. As in the Aria and other genres similar to it, the composer has no trouble in creating accompaniments that move with a life of their own, and here the prime inspiration is the Chromatic

Fourth (see above, p. 43). It too is paraphrased, so that a simple descent G F♯ F E E♭ D can become the lines shown in Example 21. This weaving of an old thread may have been so familiar that it had become second nature to Bach, who is able effortlessly to continue with it in the second half and so create a consistent and eloquent accompaniment. What emerges from Example 21 is that how ever affecting the listener finds the quite extraordinary right-hand melody of this variation to be, it is floating above counterpoint which can only be the result of careful and thoughtful ingenuity. Such concentration of the Chromatic Fourth is not only exceptional but conceived to be as stirring in its rising form as lugubrious in its falling.

Example 21   Variation No. 25

(a) Bass bb. 1–4

(b) Tenor and bass from b. 9

Brackets show the Chromatic Fourth, mostly paraphrased with a 'dragging motif'

The beauty and dark passion of No. 25 are fascinating in another respect: they raise again the question whether music expresses and arouses emotion or is really doing something else. Of course it delights in a variety of ways, and of course with a text or programme of some kind, the plaintive, even plangent, melody of No. 25 would be put to good use. But perhaps it is plaintive or plangent only by association, and what it is doing here is also something much more purely musical: realizing the potential of a harmonic framework to take immensely different shapes and involve us in the sound of its melodic embellishments. This particular one is 'sad', while the next, No. 26, is 'happy'. Yet neither need be viewed so, even if the pleasure of hearing or playing them stirs one to use such words from time to time.

## Variation 26

The exuberance of the bubbling line, in right or left hand, cannot be missed, but nor should the left hand's simple chords, either at the beginning or when they migrate to the right hand. For buried in them is a very charming sarabande, indeed a simpler exposition of the harmonies of the *Goldberg* bass-theme than the Aria itself, and not very different from some of Handel's sarabandes. Example 22 shows the opening of the left hand, arranged with harmonies that are implied rather than stated. Note that the arrangement preserves the two chords at the end of a sarabande phrase. Any such 'realization' suggests not only how curiously melodious the harmonies themselves of the *Goldberg Variations* are but how un-explicit it all is. The bubbling counterpoint is very distracting, and it surely says something about J. S. Bach that in No. 26, a rather sensuous *sarabande grave* is almost hidden from view. In general style, this sarabande recalls that of the Cello Suite in D major, BWV 1012.

Example 22    Variation No. 26, bb. 1–8, harmonized as a sarabande

The composer added grace-notes or appoggiature as to some of the chords in his copy, confirming the idea that what we have here is an elegant and *affettuoso* French sarabande – but heard against a runaway, fast-turning motif that migrates and inverts, eventually overtaking the sarabande and brushing it aside in the scramble to the final cadence. Note how the second half begins with a double inversion: the left and right hands are now reversed, and the semiquaver pattern is turned upside down.

By now, the two-manual 'arabesque' has separated the two hands by giving them different, even opposing, lines, and as such has found yet another way to use the two manuals on the day's new harpsichords. The next two variations continue to survey the possibilities.

## Variation 27

The canon at the ninth uses two manuals in order only to distinguish the two canonic lines, for the hands do not cross. There are some one-bar phrases but they always pass to a longer one, as if making a structural crescendo. The subjects are mainly smooth and conjunct, their countersubject detached and leaping, and so somewhat resemble those of the first two canons. The second half inverts freely some material from the first.

The two lines are notable in being all that there is: this canon has no bass-line and is a pure round. In performance, it has the effect of a little interlude before the final dash, but for the composer it must have offered various challenges, in particular how to follow the contours of the *Goldberg* theme when only some of its notes could be made to appear on main beats – writing a canon above a bass-line did, after all, allow the bass to trace the theme. This is now rather lost sight of as each of the four phrases progresses, and there is no true relative cadence in the second half.

Nevertheless, there is a graceful ingenuity about the piece, of which the last seven bars in particular have 'This is a canon' written all over them. Note that for each section, the voice that ends first adds a cadential phrase to accompany the other. This happens too in the *Canonic Variations* (where there is a bass-line) and the *Art of Fugue* (where there is not), while in the *Musical Offering* several canons are left so that either they require a cadence to be conjectured or they remain *canones perpetui*. Even in this little detail, therefore, the composer in his maturity was surveying all the possibilities across his different works.

## Variation 28

The crossed hands make two manuals advisable for this variation, and it seems likely that the single-manual *tutti* was being held back for the last two movements. This would be assuming that the composer was writing with a concert rhetoric (sense of climax) in mind, as too might be suggested by the *Goldberg*'s conceptual scheme – the groups of three – rather breaking down at this point. Despite the fireworks, there is a very cool calculation in the use of three distinct ideas in this variation: the trill, the left-hand quavers, and the invertible semiquavers of b. 9. The semiquaver motif heard in recurrent passages around the middle and end of each half could have appeared in any of the two-manual variations, and they too follow the bass-theme fairly literally.

Naturally, for listener and player the movement is dominated by its string of written-out trills, a very striking gesture. Not the least striking thing about them is that for most of the time, they function as embellished inner pedal-points even when they are doubled – these are not consecutive trills as can be found in earlier melodies of Bach, as for example in the Six Sonatas for Organ. Rather, again they seem prophetic of inner trills in much later piano music, being more interestingly detailed than those of a recently published Passacaglia of J. C. F. Fischer (in *Musicalischer Parnassus*, Augsburg, 1738). See Example 23. Not that Bach needed to rely on Fischer or any of *his* predecessors going back to Frescobaldi, but he is reported as admiring Fischer, and in general, the ideas dominating No. 28, and Nos. 20 and 23, might well have been consciously adopted from the current literature. (Fischer's trills are found in other 'southern organ music'.) While No. 28 keeps the idea of a trilled inner pedal-point found in Fischer and elsewhere, to omit the first of each eight notes gives a new impetus to the music. To double the trills in sixth and tenths is a gesture also taken further here than elsewhere, both contributing to a sense of climax and affording the fourth finger some fine exercises.

Example 23

(a) J. C. F. Fischer, *Musicalischer Parnassus* (Augsburg, 1738),
   final movement

(b) Variation No. 28, opening. Perhaps the beaming of the left
   hand, compared with quite similar figures in Nos. 1, 5 and 20,
   means to indicate a marked *détaché*.

## Variation 29

Uniquely for the *Goldberg*, this movement follows on the last in much
the same tempo and with much the same *Affekt*. Both are brilliant and
clearly climactic, and neither is as symmetrical as earlier variations in the
way its material recurs and re-combines.

Whether the notation of the splendid No. 29 assumes two manuals,
and thus an effect more delicate than could be achieved on the single-
manual *tutti*, is not certain. A single-manual *tutti* is possible for every
note-pattern in the variation, including the chopping chords of b. 1 especially if each of them is shared between the two hands, although that
is not suggested by the notation. Perhaps there are genuinely alterna-
tive ways of playing No. 29. One of them is more 'abstract', in that the

variation may be merely demonstrating yet another way to use the two manuals of a modern harpsichord, therefore without any sense of increasing tension; the other is more practical, with the variation excitedly following straight on No. 28, and serving together with No. 30 as the *tutti* climax to the work. Public performance must always have favoured the latter.

The 'slow multiple trill' of bb. 1ff. if the chords are divided between the hands is not found in Scarlatti quite in this form and might not have seemed to an Italian composer a suitable idea for keyboard music, whereas the alternating triplets (from b. 11) more clearly are. The idea of alternating chords must have seemed more suitable for concertos (see the oboes in the first bar of Brandenburg Concerto No. 1) and one would not be surprised to meet them in keyboard transcriptions of Italian concertos. Amongst the two-hand techniques more specifically suited to keyboards but which Bach does not use are repeated notes (as in Rameau's Variations on a Gavotte in A minor) and repeated chords (as in the transcribed Organ Concerto in G major, BWV 592).

That Nos. 28 and 29 are conceptually paired is also suggested by their opposing figuration – semiquavers where there were demisemiquavers, triplets where there were twos, and similar-but-different ways of treating the chromatic inflection halfway through each of the second halves. It is tempting for the player to vary the articulation more in No. 29, with clearly distinguished *détaché* semiquavers and *legato* quavers at key moments. In a concert, a quick succession of variations itself produces tension, and from No. 25 onwards – which opens with a minor chord cancelling the previous variation and ends with a note picked up in the next – it seems natural to play them so.

## Variation 30

In performance, the festive character of the last variation is obvious. Even the little upbeat announces that something different is happening here – it is the first and only one – and I should think that wittingly or not, the listener also senses the presence of the *Goldberg* bass at its rightful place in each bar. It is easy to be very enthusiastic about this movement, the singing lines of it, the rich four-part harmony (not heard before so fully), the four-bar phrases held together and as if inevitable. In these very respects, No. 30 recalls the final variation of the early *Aria variata* in A minor (see above, p. 39), and in function, style and figuration, they have not a little in common.

In serving rather like a chorale at the end of a Leipzig cantata in which all the performers would join – but now more high-spiritedly[4] – the last variation is the most allusive of all. It is far less predictable than the *Aria variata* finale, because it uses other melodies – for example, in b. 14 an unusual moment arises because the alto is quoting a song of the day. This is because No. 30 is a medley or 'Quodlibet' ('what you please') and as such alludes to a long tradition, even probably family tradition: making music by singing successively or simultaneously various popular tunes, often with racy texts. Not least because of a description in Michael Praetorius's *Syntagma musicum* (vol. III 1618), quodlibets were common knowledge in Germany and, as Bach's relative J. G. Walther pointed out in his *Lexicon* (Leipzig, 1732), were often jokey. From what Philipp Emanuel had told him, J. N. Forkel reported in 1802 that Bach family members would meet and sing quodlibets and 'laugh heartily', but judging by examples given in Hilgenfeldt's Bach biography of 1850 showing how five Lutheran chorales could be made to fit together, such semi-improvised music-making was not necessarily frivolous.[5]

The idea of a quasi-chorale ending an extended piece is even more ironically treated in the *Peasant Cantata* of 1742 (BWV 212), where it has become a jolly bagpipe bourrée. The link between the *Goldberg* and the *Peasant Cantata* is strengthened by their sharing a theme: the opening tenor line of the Quodlibet is quoted in the cantata (in A major) after the words 'a little cuddling', and is surely suggestive. Because they are mere incipits of songs that took different forms, the tunes used in the Quodlibet have not all been conclusively identified by current researches in German popular song, nor have their words (see Schulze, 'Melodiezitate'). But one can assume from the way that certain lines stand out melodically, or simply enter after rests, that they were something like those in Example 24. Although the words given here were written into a copy of the print by someone associated with Bach's pupil J. C. Kittel, and are usually quoted today, in fact others might have been intended, especially for the first. This tune's association elsewhere with texts of farewell and festivity seems to fit better the idea of the *Goldberg* as a carefully planned cycle now coming to an end. In any case, as with tunes of this kind popular far and wide, phrases probably migrated from one song to another, and it could well be part of the fun for No. 30 (as for the *Peasant Cantata*) to have the player search for them. Once again, the idea is not so very different from something found elsewhere in mature Bach: the 'Search and ye shall find' canons in the *Musical Offering*.

Example 24    Incipits in Variation No. 30

Ich  bin  so  lang nicht bei  dir ge-west

Kraut   und   Rü - ben   ha - ben   mich ver - trie - ben

or

## Texts:

Ich bin so lang nicht bei dir gewest
I have been so long away from you

Kraut und Rüben haben mich vertrieben
Cabbage and beets have driven me away

Quite apart from the way that it manages to develop one particular motif as if independently of the tunes (the little dactyl first heard in b. 1), the Quodlibet also contains an important and purely musical allusion. The tune called here 'Kraut und Rüben' begins much like the *Bergamasca* (also in G major) by Girolamo Frescobaldi in *Fiori musicali* of 1635, a book known to Bach. See Example 25. Frescobaldi too used both of its phrases in various counterpoints at various times in the piece, much more loosely than in the strict sixteen-bar structure of the Quodlibet but not in principle unlike it. Several northern organists of the seventeenth century used the *Bergamasca*, including Sweelinck, Scheidt and Buxtehude, and although the last composer's setting, *La Capricciosa* BuxWV 250, is not known to have been familiar to Bach, or to have existed in only its surviving form, it does have some striking things in common with the *Goldberg*. Its theme of eight bars $(2 + 2, 2 + 2)$ and its thirty-two variations, all in G major and each of them (rather simplistically) developing its particular motif, may well be playing with multiples of two.

Example 25  Frescobaldi, *Bergamasca* from *Fiori musicali* (Venice, 1635), end

(a) line 1 of original melody
(b) line 2
(c) a countersubject

For a mature composer, however, a more inspiring model for much of the *Goldberg*'s content in general would have been Frescobaldi's *Bergamasca*, where the handling of imitation, different themes, beautiful harmonic turns, natural melodiousness, contrapuntal combination and changes of metre are in their way comparable. In turn, the Quodlibet may well have gone on ringing in its composer's ears, for one hears more than passing similarities to it at various points in the *Peasant Cantata* (1742) – its cadence bars, quaver tunes and imitation in the aria 'Ach Herr Schösser', for example.

## Aria

That the repeat of the *Aria* was not written out is a reminder that any symmetry or number-play pointed out in this account of the *Goldberg* is not obtrusive or made distractingly obvious. (Even the prevailing two- and four-bar phrases are matters for private recognition.) One wonders, therefore, how many players of the time, on seeing the direction *aria da capo*, realized the various 32s involved: the number of the page, the number of the unwritten movement, and the number of bars it and the other movements contained. Perhaps they saw it as merely another rubric of the kind found after the last variation of Muffat's *Componimenti* of *c.* 1739: 'il Primo Motivo della Ciacona Da Capo'. Modern players too might not realize that if they do not repeat each half of the returning *Aria*, they are interfering with the *Goldberg*'s persistent and consistent binary patterns.

The *Goldberg*'s elusive beauty, an uncanny world not quite like any other, is reinforced by this return to the Aria. In music, no such return can have a neutral Affekt. Its melody is made to stand out by what has gone on in the last five variations, and it is likely to appear wistful or nostalgic or subdued or resigned or sad, heard on its repeat with a sense of something coming to an end, the same notes but now final.

# 4

## Questions of reception

### The first hundred years

It must surely have been the case that Wilhelm Friedemann and possibly Philipp Emanuel played the *Goldberg*, even perhaps in some kind of public performance in the various cities to which their profession took them. But documentation has not yet emerged to say where, when and how.

Emanuel's path-breaking book on keyboard playing (Part I 1753, Part II 1762) has a final chapter on improvisation in which various idiomatic keyboard figuration is illustrated, but while several examples can be found in his father's organ music (toccatas and the like), none relates closely to figural patterns in the *Goldberg*. That is strange, as the *Goldberg*'s figuration was certainly not as old-fashioned as some that Emanuel did illustrate, and it could be that he saw it as more suited to harpsichord than the fortepiano he had in mind. On the other hand, if Emanuel was involved in writing the *Comparison between Handel and Bach* published in Berlin in 1788 (Dok III, p. 927), as he very likely was, he did express admiration for the *Goldberg*, calling it a work of riches, many-sided, up-to-date and idiomatic for keyboard. The intention here was to draw a comparison to the detriment of Handel's variations, for it is clear from the Bach Obituary that Handel's success (and wealth) abroad rankled with the younger generation of Bach pupils. But since Handel's various sets of variations circulated widely, such remarks might have increased interest in Bach's one published set.

The appearance of three movements in Hawkins's history of music published in London in 1776 has already been noted, but otherwise the work drops largely from view for many decades after first publication. Such references as have been found between the Obituary (1754) and Forkel's biography (1802) include a few brief notices, as when an advertisement listing music available from the Leipzig publisher Breitkopf included the work (1770 – Dok III, p. 152). The technique of contrapuntal variation in both the *Goldberg* and *Canonic Variations*, and even the *Goldberg*'s combining of time-signatures in No. 26 (!), might have been valued highly by certain Bach-admirers in the 1770s, but if they occasionally mentioned the work in print, they gave little detail and no illustration (Dok III, pp. 213, 294). Hawkins's examples are complete and include one canon (No. 9) and fugue (No. 10) but no two-manual virtuoso movement, suggesting perhaps that either he or his source found the contrapuntally ingenious movements more interesting, even more comprehensible. Many potential buyers must have found the very appearance on the page of not a few variations quite baffling. Perhaps they were meant to.

More important are the two brief quotes given by Kirnberger in his practical theory book *Die Kunst des reinen Satzes* (1771–9), for this was a book known and perhaps used in teaching by various influential teachers, including Beethoven, it seems. But even here, the quotations hardly stand out amongst many examples of Bach's ingenuities and harmonic solutions, and although it is so that Kirnberger grasped enough to extract the *Goldberg*'s bass-theme or *Grundbass* as he called it, he gives only the first half of it and shows no sign of knowing its part in music's history. Nor does he appear alerted to the various symmetries at play.

Time and again in the later eighteenth century, it is J. S. Bach's fugal writing, particularly in the *Well-tempered Clavier* and the *Art of Fugue*, that features in the literature of various kinds, including reports of what gifted young people played (S. Wesley, Beethoven). Organists may have copied or imitated or even regularly played various groups of organ chorales, including those of *Clavierübung III*, but even a gifted pianist such as the Dresdener A. A. Klengel (1783–1852) showed his awareness of the *Goldberg* chiefly, perhaps only, by imitating its canonic techniques in much of his own work, including the *Exercises pour le piano-forte* (1841). Obviously, the piano was less likely to stay with the old repertory than was the church organ. Meanwhile, however, Forkel himself had composed some variations imitating some of the *Goldberg*'s techniques, apparently many years before his biography appeared in 1802.[1] Not great music, but in the world of Bach-admirers, perhaps the tip of an iceberg?

I suspect that if the *Goldberg* played so little a part in the piano-studies or performances of Czerny, Mendelssohn, Thalberg, Chopin and Schumann – clearly an area deserving further research – it was or would have been because its keyboard figuration appeared more dated than would counterpoint of the kind found in the *Well-tempered Clavier*, excerpts from which were not rarely heard. In public, Schumann and his wife were more likely to play piano transcriptions of chorales than anything in *Clavierübung*, which he seems to have regarded as 'exercises' or *études* in the usual sense at the time, perhaps misled by the title.[2]

In his recital tours during the 1838–48 period, Liszt included (some of?) the *Goldberg* along with other of his Bach favourites, including the *Chromatic Fantasia and Fugue*, but its impact on him has not yet been studied. As Mendelssohn and Clara Schumann too found, the *Chromatic Fantasia* was well suited not only to the piano itself but to ideas of the time on musical rhetoric and the arts of recitation. For many pianists throughout the century, the *Goldberg* must have seemed as alien to the new concert-halls as a baroque organ did to neo-gothic churches. But Brahms was not the only connoisseur of canons and similar composition, and evidently Liszt kept an interest in the *Goldberg*: one of his pupils tells of playing it to him in 1885, a work brought to her attention by the master but otherwise by then 'completely overlooked by the pianists'.[3]

Throughout this period, the various attempts at Complete Bach Editions had resulted in Bach's keyboard music being available to the discriminating buyer, particularly Hoffmeister's edition appearing in Vienna and Leipzig in 1803 (where the *Goldberg*, French Suites and *Well-Tempered Clavier* Book 2 were each divided across two volumes) and Nägeli's in Zurich in 1809. A series of re-issues by Peters in Leipzig kept the work in print, not least through Czerny's fingered edition of it appearing in 1840 and paired there with *Clavierübung II*. Particularly Czerny's publication must have been used by piano students for several generations. Finally, the Bach Society Edition (BG) of 1853 meant an incomparable authority ready to hand for connoisseurs such as Brahms, who became a subscriber to the BG from 1856 and took pains to make sure he had all the volumes. (Brahms realized too that the theme had precedents in Handel and Muffat.) The BG inspired newer perform-ing editions such as Hans Bischoff's (1880–8) and Josef Rheinberger's version for two pianos (1883), as well as the various uses to which the twentieth century put the work. These last include piano performances backed by descriptive analysis (Tovey, 1900), new adaptations for pianists (Busoni's edition, with the variations re-ordered for a greater sense of climax, 1915),[4] technical studies (Busoni's exercises based on *Goldberg* figuration, 1914), and acting as a standard-bearer, in more or less original form, for the later harpsichord revival (Landowska, Kirkpatrick).[5]

That actually playing the work in public during the nineteenth century did not accord with current tastes is confirmed by a characteristic satire of E. T. A. Hoffmann, who remarked that 'Johann Sebastian Bach's Variations' would send concert-goers packing.[6] Rather than merely returning to the Aria at the end, better would be some flamboyant improvisation based on the theme, he thought. However, by 1886, the organological expert A. J. Hipkins was 'reviving' the *Goldberg Variations* by playing some of them to the (Royal) Musical Association in London, on the harpsichord.

## Beethoven's *Diabelli Variations*

Whether the *Goldberg*'s Aria is to be seen as a sarabande-like 'general model' for the themes of variations in Beethoven's *Archduke Trio* (1811) or piano Sonata in E major, Op. 109 (1820)[7] is doubtful, for many other sets of variations were then circulating, including Handel's. The *Eroica* variations for piano (1802) and the *Thirty-two Variations in C minor* (1806) resemble the *Goldberg* in being based on a skeletal bass and/or a formulaic series of harmonies, but whether this is due to some direct influence is unclear. A better case for there being some special relationship with the *Goldberg* can be made for the *Diabelli Variations* (1819–23), if only because they both represent their composer's biggest achievements in variation form (and are so looked at by some modern pianists) and because Diabelli himself referred to 'Johann Sebastian Bach's masterpiece in the same form' in an advertisement.[8] If Beethoven was already playing a manuscript copy of the still unpublished *Well-tempered Clavier* at the age of eleven, as in 1790 E. L. Gerber said he had been (see Dok III, p. 475), it is certainly possible that printed copies of the *Goldberg* were being played here and there twenty years later, perhaps as transmitted via the publisher Breitkopf and his contacts in Vienna and elsewhere.

Details in the *Diabelli* that might suggest at least a general absorption of Bach idioms include stretto imitation (*Diabelli* Nos. 4, 6, 30) and the imitative exploring of a note-pattern (Nos. 11, 12), melismatic and/or chromatic filgree work in the minor (No. 31), original keyboard figuration (No. 6) including alternating and crossing or chopping hands (Nos. 9, 21 and 23 – compare *Goldberg* Nos. 14, 20 and 23), inventive triplet motifs (Nos. 26, 27), an *alla breve* fugue (No. 32), a triple-time fugue beginning off the beat (No. 24) and a graceful dance (minuet, No. 33). More generally, the two sets also have in common the changes and contrasts between the metre and pulse of successive variations. But none of these need go back to Bach in any direct way, even if they undoubtedly go ahead to Brahms, whose *Handel Variations* Op. 24 are generally said in the literature (though without specifics) to spring from his intimate acquaintance with the *Goldberg*, the *Diabelli* and the *Eroica* variations, as well as Handel's.

Variation No. 31 of the *Diabelli* has often been suggested[9] as an 'imitation' of the adagio variation in the *Goldberg* (No. 25), but this example suggests the weakness of such parallels. One powerful or passionate piece may remind the listener or player of another, especially when those pieces are placed at comparable points in their whole work; and two slow melodious pieces in the minor might be similar in some broad sense. But a *piano piangevole* movement at some such point near the end of a set of variations was traditional, and the very originality with which both *Diabelli* No. 31 and *Goldberg* No. 25 are worked makes more than general points hazardous. It is certainly likely that of all the movements in the *Goldberg*, No. 25 would go to the heart of a Beethoven, but this too cannot be much more than a guess.

What might be surviving in the *Diabelli* is not so much the *Goldberg's* exploration of 'abstract' keyboard patterns – this was normal with all variations from 1600 to 1800 – but the uncanny mixture between patterns that are startlingly original and those that are quite ordinary or elemental (such as scales), even verging on the banal (in Beethoven's case, matching the original waltz). The very structure of both the *Goldberg* and *Diabelli* themes is archetypal, not to say square: both contain thirty-two bars, with two exact halves each repeated, and both have four-bar phrases of a standard kind (particularly inelegant in the theme of the *Diabelli*). The music in both of them is often drawn from simple motifs, plain triads and everyday rhythms, all of which supply material for unusual music of great originality and expressiveness. Especially in Beethoven's case, it is as if a composer had felt challenged to rise above the ordinary by applying it extraordinarily. Perhaps this is so for both composers: a much used formulaic bass inspiring Bach, a tacky waltz of Diabelli inspiring Beethoven, both of them to otherwise unknown realms of musical imagination.

## Some modern theories

Since the *Goldberg*'s idiosyncratic beauty cannot be admired *ad infinitum*, and since the originality of its strategy and tactics – its organization and its bar-by-bar composition – is so pronounced, it has often become the focus for analyses and intepretations of a rarefied, theoretical kind. In this, it will sometimes be joined by similar work on other mature works of Bach, particularly the *Musical Offering*, *Canonic Variations* and *Art of Fugue*, all of which are open to a hermeneutic that is partly musical (based on analysis of technicalities) and partly extra-musical (drawing on ideas from other realms). Particularly tempting in recent times have been the searches either for allegorical or so-called symbolic meanings in Bach (as in the harmony of *canones*, i.e. 'rules') or for detailed analyses at both tactical and strategic levels (i.e. of individual motifs and overall structure).[10]

It is not always clear from such studies whether Bach is being claimed to be wittingly engaged in symbolic and other significances or whether these are ineluctable elements of any music called profound. But it is probably fair to regard the studies as intending somehow to match the 'unearthly' quality that is heard in the music itself, or perhaps in any good music. If the triad itself can be interpreted theologically (the trias as the Trinity, three-in-one, minor an 'inversion' of major as grief is of joy), so might all inspiring music (Browne's 'something in it of Divinity'). Ideas change with the times, and theological interpretations are now less likely than cognitive or mechanistic or semiotic or even sociological.

Two interpretations specific to the *Goldberg* and published in the last twenty years can stand here for others written in English, German or other languages, usually as part of an approach to the keyboard works of Bach's last decade, works which obviously inhabit a musical world different (remoter?) from that of most instrumental music of the time. These two interpretations speak in turn of the *Goldberg*'s 'cosmological allegory' (Humphreys, 1984–5) and its 'rhetorico-musical structure' (Street, 1987) and thus represent the searches for symbolic or structural significances in music that is not only without words (and thus clear pointers to its 'meaning') but is unique in conception and accomplishment.

The first of these is based primarily on two suppositions: that in the *Goldberg* there is a 'single unifying principle which explains Bach's design', and that the 'Fourteen Canons' BWV 1087 bear on this 'organisational principle behind the work' – although, since the 'Fourteen Canons' are said to 'form a link' with various 'numerological structures' based on 14 (= bach) and 41 (= jsbach) in other late works, their bearing specifically on the *Goldberg* seems to be no more than slight. Instead, an attempt is made to show the larger work to possess not merely various symmetries achieved in purely musical terms, but an altogether bigger agenda, 'an allegorical scheme' from another realm, nothing less than 'an ascent through the nine spheres of Ptolemaic cosmology'. This is achieved in the *Goldberg*

> partly through the symbolism of the nine canons, but principally through the medium of the great international sign-language of word-painting and oratorical devices which Bach was heir to, and in which his vocal music is steeped. (Humphreys, p. 26)

Thus the thirty variations (but not the thirty-two movements) are explained as containing three cycles: the canon cycle (nine canons whose time-signatures provide all nine possible pairings of the digits 2, 3 and 4, as in 2/4, 3/8 and so on), the 'planet cycle' (movements 1, 2, 4, 7, 10, 13, 16, 19, 22, 25, 28, 30) and the 'virtuoso cycle' (nos. 5, 8, 11, 14, 17, 20, 23, 26, 29). What are called the 'oratorical devices' permitting such an interpretation are the associations, belonging primarily to music with words, between words and certain musical motifs or characteristics – as a rising allegro melody serves the words 'and he arose'.

The ruling idea of the hypothesis is that nine 'planet cycle' variations (i.e. apparently excluding Nos. 1 and 2) 'picture each of the nine spheres in turn' by musical means. These might be summarily described as follows:

No. 4      Earth (hemiolas suggest earthly change and decay)

No. 7      Moon (here, a transient, inconstant gigue)

No. 10    Mercury ('Mercury stands beating his wings on the mordent')

No. 13    Venus (elegant, graceful, delicate, refined, sensitive; *tendresse*)

No. 16    Sun (the French style, regal)

No. 19    Mars (a battle piece with writhing and raging semiquavers)

No. 22    Jupiter (in *alla breve* or antique style, patriarchal)

No. 25    Saturn (melancholy intimations of transience and mortality)

No. 28    Fixed stars (twinkling, so that theme-inversion = star-reflection)

As often with interpretations of Bach, this one claims to have practical consequences, such that 'conventional approaches to a few variations may be in need of revision'. Thus the syncopations of No. 19 have to be interpreted as 'disruptive' or aggressive, the *alla breve* No. 22 as not 'fast, spiky' but 'smooth, solemn'.

A problem is that every one of these nine – to say nothing of the other cycles as described – requires some special pleading and a partial characterization, i.e. some but not all elements in the musical makeup of a variation have been selected to parallel as best they can partially selected attributes of a planet. Which planet corresponds to which variation may depend on arbitrary attribution in both the music and the planet itself. For example, are these the commonly accepted attributes of Venus? Or if No. 16 is sun-like, so presumably must be the B minor Ouverture in *Clavierübung II*, in which case what is the Italian Concerto in the same volume – the moon? (What does 'is' mean?) If not, one has to show that symbolisms operate only in certain conditions, just as one needs to explain why they operate in one way and not another. For example, if No. 22 really is patriarchal in its *alla breve* counterpoint, why is this expressed so briefly in the *Goldberg* – because Zeus was something of a fly-by-night character? And why this particular *alla breve* movement and not the other two composed in this style? Why nine planets and not nine muses, with e.g. Clio for one or other of the *Goldberg* movements *in stile antico*?

It would be possible to propose and justify such alternatives, no doubt, but there would still be two problems. The first is, what in any case is the verb, what are the movements *doing*? In such interpretations, are the movements being said to parallel, correspond to, evoke, invoke, suggest, express, be expressive of, symbolize, articulate, intone? All or any of these? The second problem is, Where does it all stop? For a cantata text to have a specific sentiment or allusion marked by a particular musical detail is for music to draw attention, by conventional means, to that sentiment or allusion. But even then, there is a limit to what it can evoke – for example, a rising allegro melody for 'he hath put down the mighty' would need further explanation. Without a text or context there is nothing to go on.

The second approach, from rhetoric, aims to show that in taking 'its ultimate inspiration from Quintilian's *Institutio oratoria*, the *Goldberg Variations* actually 'represent Bach's definitive defence of [against] Scheibe's criticisms', doing so better than his recent volume of organ music, *Clavierübung III*. (J. A. Scheibe had published reviews in 1737 and 1739 criticizing Bach for excessive and unnatural artifice. Quintilian was a first-century rhetorician mentioned in the preface to Vetter's book of chorales referred to on p. 103 below, note 1 (Introduction), and author of a treatise still taught in outline in eighteenth-century German schools.) The approach assumes that 'in the absence of an obvious *raison d'être* for the *Goldberg*', one has to be supplied, and that the work can be read in a quasi-programmatic way.

Thus, apparently following Quintilian's advice that in giving a speech, one finds the best words for it in the subject-matter itself, Bach adopts variation form as a 'perfect example of formal economy', and otherwise, his turning to variation form is hard to explain. According to Quintilian's advice, thoughts are to be ordered and linked coherently; so the variations are grouped and planned, all connected by the *Goldberg* bass. Then, the various multiples and powers of two in evidence throughout the work 'have a strong connection with certain passages from Plato's *Timaeus*', where the 'world-soul' is represented by squares and cubes of two and three. At the same time, rhetorical *figurae* can be easily discerned in the music, so that the 'proliferation of anabasis–catabasis figures' in

No. 14 (i.e. the rising and falling patterns) ensures 'that the audience is transported by admiration', as Quintilian recommends. Similarly, No. 15 'concludes the *narratio* by virtue of its existence as a species of *peroratio*', while the canon at the ninth is 'the apotheosis of the work . . . a consummate union of dualistic ideas' in its two parts without bass.

Much of this is as harmless as it is hilarious, but in being typical of such claims about Bach, the real concern is its apparent conviction not only that to be rhetorically effective one needs (and Bach needed?) to know rhetoric, but that the written rules of rhetoric in some way directly explain musical issues. Thus, Variation No. 1 'follows immediately on the theme' because Quintilian advised that the transition from the *exordium* (Aria) 'be smooth yet distinct'. Or, the first canon 'obeys Quintilian's instructions to say nothing contrary to nature'. Or, since Bach is throughout defending himself against Scheibe, he introduces a reference to BACH (b♭ a c b♮) in the course of Variation No. 6 (over bb. 11–13). Or, since the *Goldberg* contains both major and minor variations, they reflect Quintilian's remarks on the need for different facts, to be 'united with what precedes and follows'. Similarly, the opening Aria is as it is because in order to answer Scheibe's accusations, Bach needed to begin his rhetorical address with a 'galant miniature as his theme' and show that he could write such music. And the final Quodlibet not only 'turns Scheibe into the butt of Bach's humour' but contains a quotation from the old song 'L'homme armé' (*sic*).

Unfortunately for its author, this essay's whole approach from Quintilian is modelled on a previous and similar reading of the *Musical Offering* that was never more than conjectural, unilluminating, and irrelevant. Outside certain corners of musicology such work is soon recognized as engaging in no more than 'naive and fanciful analogies', in the words of one historian of rhetoric.[11]

# Notes

## Introduction

1 The collection of varied chorales *Musicalische Kirch- und Haussgötzlichkeit*, 2 vols. (Leipzig, 1709 and 1713).

2 Similarly, if Goldberg had been a 'pupil of Bach', as sometimes claimed (see Dok III, p. 624), one could imagine this to mean a pupil of Friedemann in Dresden as much as of Sebastian in Leizpig.

3 This was the church with which the young Handel had been associated, through his teacher Friedrich Wilhelm Zachow.

4 The 'earlier' versions of Partitas Nos. 3 and 6 in the *Anna Magdalena Book* had a compass of C–c''' only and were thus expanded for the published version. C–c''' is also the compass of most of the fugues of the *Art of Fugue*, as if this were the classic fugue-range – as indeed it is.

## 1 Background and genesis

1 The *New Bach Edition* of the *Anna Magdalena Book* by Georg von Dadelsen (NBA vol. V/4) calls them 'Partitas', which is misleading.

2 Significantly, the one 2/4 movement in the solo violin works is found in an Italianate sonata: the A minor Fugue (Sonata, BWV 1003), which has a short subject of the kind called *attacca*.

3 Allegro used for the first movement of a transcribed Vivaldi concerto (BWV 975) cannot mean anything very lively, rather a spacious and deliberate 2/4, like the first movement of Bach's Italian Concerto.

4 There is an extant version of the Italian Concerto's first movement that is simpler, more galant, more commonplace – and more like a transcription, without manual-changes, of an Italian concerto. But because it is so, one need not conclude that it 'transmits . . . an early version', as suggested in Beisswenger, 'An Early Version': it could be an unauthorized adaptation.

5 The price was 3 reichsthaler. In 1740 in Leipzig, Lorenz Mizler's translation of Fux's *Gradus ad parnassum* was advertised at 2 reichsthaler, in 1751 the first edition of the *Kunst der Fuge* sold for 5, the second edition for 4. With apparently the same currency in the same area, a small but new clavichord in 1745 need cost only 10 reichsthaler (see Dähnert, 'Hildebrandt', p. 231).

6 An idea developed in Breig, 'Goldberg'. In a not dissimilar way, it has been argued that 'the last five of the Diabelli Variations [by 1823] expand the possibilities of the work beyond anything Beethoven envisioned in the spring of 1819' – Kindermann, *Diabelli*, p. 114.

7 See Tomita, 'Early Drafts'. It is not unknown for copyists to simplify figuration, of course.

8 Whether the composer planned the *Art of Fugue* with the fugue *in stile francese* as the centre point, and whether he labelled it so, are unclear. Nevertheless, though called 'Contrapunctus 6' in the posthumous edition, in the extant autograph it is No. 7 of thirteen fugues, and the interspersed canons may not have been intended to remain where they are.

9 Of *Clavierübung III*, Butler aptly remarks in *Making of a Print*, p. 80: 'Bach, as publisher, would have had to be in attendance while the work was going through the press, keeping an eye on the printing and supervising corrections made to the text.' This was in Leipzig; for the *Goldberg*, presumably being engraved in Nuremberg, any instructions would have had to be given some other way.

10 Used in E major for the subject of the Fugue BWV 878 in the *Well-tempered Clavier* Book 2, probably but not certainly before these canons. As Wolff, 'Handexemplar', implies, the source of Fux's treatise was probably the translation of it by Bach's student Lorenz Mizler (see note 5).

11 That is, as other composers familar with it did not – a fact often taken to be more of a credit to Bach (for example, in Wolff, 'Handexemplar') than might be justified.

## 2 Overall shape

1 But accepted by Spitta, *Bach*, vol. I, pp. 126–7 and KB, p. 110.

2 Perhaps with reference to another Raison theme for the second half: see Williams, *Organ Music*, p. 256.

3 'Perhaps', because the *piano* echoes do not absolutely require a second manual.

4 As required on the title-page of the *Two-part Inventions*, presumably as advice for the young Wilhelm Friedemann.

## 3 The movements

1 Excerpt in NBA vol. V/2 KB, p. 110. Spitta (*Bach*, vol. I, p. 126) also finds traces of J. C. Bach's variations in the *Aria variata* in A minor, BWV 989.
2 According to Quantz, *Versuch*, p. 271.
3 This could well mean that the left hand should read b′ at the beginning of b. 29 and c′ at the same point in b. 30. (The engraving is not entirely reliable in No. 17 at this point.)
4 Writing in 1900, Tovey was surely right in saying (if somewhat obscurely) that in the Quodlibet, 'we have no possible doubt that Bach is writing in a mood which an ordinary modern composer would be likely to regard as one of dangerous high spirits' ('Goldberg', p. 35). Dangerous because a more portentous ending would be more to the taste of the then modern composer?
5 Hilgenfeldt's biography (q.v.) was popular over the years that Wagner was composing *Die Meistersinger*, and it is not out of the question that the combination of themes in that opera was a witting allusion to such late medieval practice amongst German musicians, in Hans Sachs's Nuremberg as in Bach's Eisenach and Wagner's Leipzig.

## 4 Questions of reception

1 See Tovey, 'Goldberg', for brief description and excerpts.
2 See Plantinga, *Schumann*, pp. 87, 146.
3 See Jerger, *Liszt*, p. 167.
4 See Zenck, 'Bach, der Progressive'. Note that Busoni's idea, doubtless influenced by the *Diabelli* and other variation-sets, was foreshadowed by E. T. A. Hoffmann, referred to below (note 6).
5 Landowska's habit of repeating not the whole second half but only the last few bars is less an allusion to the *petite reprise* of French classical composers, perhaps, than a necessity imposed by the length of the side of a 78 rpm recording.
6 *Allgemeine musikalische Zeitung* 12 (1810), cols. 825ff. The remarks are aimed at certain fashionable kinds of concert of the day, and the *Goldberg* is not referred to by name.
7 See Kindermann, 'Bach', p. 356. The sarabande-like nature of any such variation-themes, in a slow and 'serious' triple time, may well be a reaction to the usual piano variations of the day.
8 See Tovey, 'Goldberg', p. 124. The reference certainly suggests not only respect for the *Goldberg* but that it may have been generally familiar, at least amongst connoisseurs.

9 E.g. in Rosen, *Classical Style*, p. 439. No. 31 was probably the last variation to be composed (Kindermann, 'Diabelli', p. 60).

10 As an instance of the first: Eric Chafe, 'Allegorical Music: The Symbolism of Tonal Language in the Bach Canons', *Journal of Musicology* 3 (1984), pp. 340–62. And of the second: articles in *Musik-Konzepte* 42 (1985).

11 Vickers, *Defence of Rhetoric*, p. 374. The work in question, a *ne plus ultra* of such groundless speculation, is Ursula Kirkendale, 'The Source for Bach's *Musical Offering*', *Journal of the American Musicological Society* 33 (1980), pp. 88–141.

# Bibliography

Alain, Olivier, 'Un supplément inédit aux Variations Goldberg de J. S. Bach', *Revue de musicologie* 61/2 (1975), pp. 243–94

Bach, Carl Philipp Emanuel, *Versuch über die wahre Art das Clavier zu spielen*, 2 vols. (Berlin, 1753, 1762)

Beisswenger, Kirsten, 'An Early Version of the First Movement of the *Italian Concerto* BWV 971 from the Scholz Collection?', in Daniel R. Melamed, ed., *Bach Studies* 2 (Cambridge: Cambridge University Press, 1995), pp. 1–19

Bloom, Harold, *The Western Canon: The Books and School of the Ages* (New York: Harcourt Brace, 1994)

Breig, Werner, 'Bachs Goldberg-Variationen als zyklisches Werk', *Archiv für Musikwissenschaft* 32 (1975), pp. 243–65

Butler, Gregory, 'The Engraving of J. S. Bach's Six Partitas', *Journal of Musicological Research* 7 (1986), pp. 3–27

'Neues zur Datierung der Goldberg-Variationen', *Bach-Jahrbuch* 74 (1988), pp. 219–23

*Bach's Clavier-Übung III: The Making of a Print* (Durham, NC: Duke University Press, 1990)

Dähnert, Ulrich, *Der Orgel- und Instrumentenbauer Zacharias Hildebrandt* (Leipzig: Breitkopf & Härtel, 1962)

Elster, Peter, 'Anmerkungen zur Aria der sogenannten Goldbergvariationen BWV 988. Bachs Bearbeitung eines französischen Menuetts', in Winfried Hoffmann and Armin Schneiderheinze, eds., *Bericht über die Wissenschaftliche Konferenz zum V. Internationalen Bachfest 1985* (Leipzig: DVfM, 1988), pp. 259–67

Emery, Walter, in NBA vol. V/2 KB, pp. 137ff., 141, 143f.

Forkel, J[ohann] N[ikolaus], *Über Johann Sebastian Bachs Leben, Kunst und Kunstwerke. Für patriotische Verehrer echter musikalischer Kunst* (Leipzig: Hoffmeister & Kühnel, 1802)

Hawkins, John, *A General History of the Science and Practice of Music*, vol. III (London: Payne, 1776), pp. 256–58

Hilgenfeldt, C[arl] L[udwig], *Johann Sebastian Bach's Leben, Wirken und Werke* (Leipzig: Hofmeister, 1850), appendices

Humphreys, David, 'More on the Cosmological Allegory in Bach's Goldberg Variations', *Soundings* 12 (1984–5), pp. 25–45

Jerger, Wilhelm, ed., *The Piano Master Classes of Franz Liszt 1884–1886* (Bloomington, IN: Indiana University Press, 1996)

Kindermann, William, *Beethoven's Diabelli Variations* (Oxford: Clarendon, 1987)

'Bach und Beethoven', in Michael Heinemann and Hans-Joachim Hinrichsen, eds., *Bach und die Nachwelt*, vol. I (Laaber: Laaber Verlag, 1997), pp. 351–77

Kobayashi, Yoshitake, 'Zur Chronologie der Spätwerke Johann Sebastian Bachs. Kompositions- und Aufführungstätigkeit von 1736 bis 1750', *Bach-Jahrbuch* 74 (1988), pp. 7–72

Plantinga, Leon B., *Schumann as Critic* (New York: Da Capo, 1976)

Quantz, Johann Joachim, *Versuch einer Anweisung, die Flöte traversière zu spielen* (Berlin, 1752)

Rosen, Charles, *The Classical Style: Haydn, Mozart, Beethoven* (New York: Norton, 1972)

Schulenberg, David, *The Keyboard Music of J. S. Bach* (New York: Schirmer, 1992)

Schulze, Hans-Joachim, 'Melodiezitate und Mehrtextigkeit in der Bauern-kantate und in den Goldbergvariationen', *Bach-Jahrbuch* 62 (1976), pp. 58–72

'Notizen zu Bachs Quodlibets', *Bach-Jahrbuch* 80 (1994), pp. 171–5

Spitta, Philipp, *Johann Sebastian Bach*, 2 vols. (Leipzig: Breitkopf, 1873, 1880)

Street, Alan, 'The Rhetorico-musical Structure of the "Goldberg" Variations: Bach's *Clavierübung IV* and the *Institutio oratoria* of Quintilian', *Music Analysis* 6 (1987), pp. 89–131

Tomita, Yo, 'Bach and his Early Drafts', *BACH Journal of the Riemenschneider Bach Institute* 30/2 (1999), pp. 49–72

Tovey, Donald Francis, 'Bach: Goldberg Variations', *Essays in Musical Analysis: Chamber Music*, ed. Hubert J. Foss (London: Oxford University Press, 1944), pp. 28–73

Vickers, Brian, *In Defence of Rhetoric* (Oxford: Clarendon, 1988)

Williams, Peter, *The Organ Music of J. S. Bach, vol. I: Preludes [etc.]* (Cambridge: Cambridge University Press, 1980)

Wolff, Christoph, 'Bach's Handexemplar of the Goldberg Variations: A New Source', *Journal of the American Musicological Society* 29 (1976), pp. 224–41

   *Bach: Essays on his Life and Music* (Cambridge, MA: Harvard University Press, 1991), pp. 162ff., 189ff., 347ff.

Zenck, Martin, ' "Bach, der Progressive". Die Goldberg-Variationen in der Perspektive von Beethovens Diabelli-Variationen', *Musik-Konzepte* 42 (1985), pp. 29–92

# Index